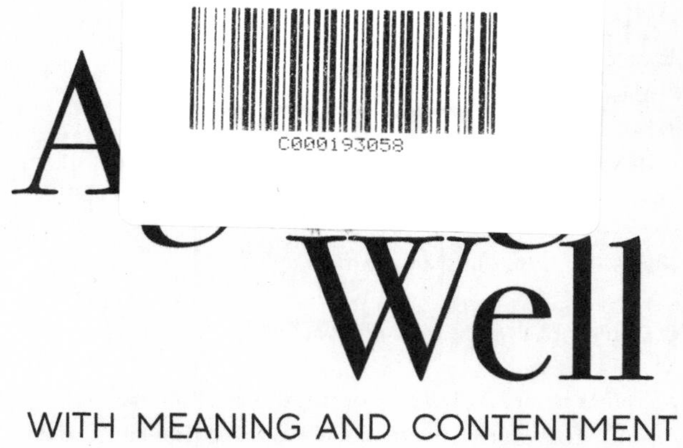

WITH MEANING AND CONTENTMENT

FRANCIS MACNAB

Published by:
Wilkinson Publishing Pty Ltd
ACN 006 042 173
Level 4, 2 Collins St Melbourne, Victoria, Australia 3000
Ph: +61 3 9654 5446
www.wilkinsonpublishing.com.au

A catalogue record for this book is available from the National Library of Australia

Planned date of publication: 05-2020
Title: Ageing Well
ISBN(s): 9781925642971: Printed – Paperback

Cover layout based on an original design by Alicia Freile, Tango Media Pty Ltd.

Contents

AGEING WELL

Chapter 1

Finding Meaning

I find myself in new spiritual, emotional, and psychological territory. It is called older age. Like everyone, I find it helps to understand where I have come from, where I want to be, and how to get there. And perhaps most importantly, what we all need to flourish and thrive rather than just survive in our later years.

As I reflect on my life as it is, I am physically fit, mentally alert, moods stable, discerning about relationships, financially nervous as always and oscillating between optimism and pessimism about today's world. A regular reader of the obituaries in the daily newspapers, easily bored by irrelevant sermons and a depleted religion, a regular observer of the tram drivers pushing the high-speed button on every corner. A proven performer, successful negotiator, a writer of books, an original thinker, still full of energy and vitality, ready to live another life.

FOLLOWING A PASSION

Throughout my life, psychology and psychoanalysis have fired my curiosity and searching. I have practised throughout some sixty years in the world of psychotherapy. This is longer than many live. Some will say I have spent too much time with the downcast and depressed, but that simply grabs a superficial stereotype. It misses the large numbers of people I have seen who tell me how they collided with the traumas of life and transcended them. How they found they had carried the ticket of low self-esteem in their pockets for decades and in the last stages of their life decided to throw that ticket away and embrace a way of life that was exciting to them and unbelievable to those who had known them in their earlier life.

I am all too aware of my mistakes, aware that my regrets are no help now. I notice I still miss the psychological turning points. Although I have heard a voice saying 'if possible, do a U-turn', I drive on, assured in myself that I know where I should be going. With my experience of helping others live their lives, I could be expected to look to these last years with considerable wisdom. But I am still making many of the same mistakes.

CREATING JOY

You may well ask: how do I fill my time? I find an important aspect of growing older is to recognise the importance of finding and creating joy. I can often be found at my desk. You might observe me beginning to draw lines on a page. Call it doodling if you like. But as I continue, the lines begin to form the shape of a face. A few more touches with the pen this way or that, and the face gathers expression of emotion, softness, searching, gentleness, and curiosity. I recognise someone in this face. Someone known, never known, or wished they were unknown. The face of the unknown becomes a creation of someone perhaps known, but not known. The achievement of this clumsy creation evokes a sense of joy.

I also find joy in writing words. Something in me becomes aroused by these words. They are not words of poetry or of science, nor the words of request or demand. Instead, they become just words that dangle like fruit on the tree. I take words and they begin to form a theme, not premeditated, but rather streams of consciousness, a flow of words. Move one word, change another, the theme takes its shape, tells its story. As strange as this might seem, this clumsy creation creates a sense of joy.

FULFILLING MOMENTS

Another source of joy is to be found as I walk the streets near my home. With my thoughts wandering, I turn a corner. There before me, a person I had not seen for five or more years. They were always a good presence in times past, but over prior years, have become only a whisper of a presence. My mind wonders about that good presence, where it currently makes itself known. Suddenly it is present. This unsought creation evokes a great sense of joy.

Out of nowhere, there is something, a blank page, or a face. Out of a mind of random thoughts, a theme. In a street empty for years, a person appears. The joy gives shape to what will follow. What will follow? One presence brings joy. At another time, that presence may have elicited fear. An obituary speaks of many joys of the past, joys of remembering, and joys of gratitude. Friendly faces step out of the past into the distressed mind-space, where the emotion of joy is mixed with grief. The present and the past come together, and create a wondering about a future where joy will be present once more.

MANAGING MOODS

Like everyone, I am at the mercy of my moods. I recognise that from early childhood, we learn how 'to do' bad moods. Our negative emotions collude with negative cognitions. They cause us to believe people are against us, that we are no good, and life today is messy and miserable. I also notice my moods being affected by people and events in the small zones of my life, as well as in events in the wider world.

A major task is to sustain a balanced mood not only in the contexts of people and events, but also in the context of mind states, body chemistry, and in the contexts of my hopes, enjoyments, and resentments. In my most difficult and darkest moments, the breeze blows the leaves, and sunshine floods into my room. We know these moments and they pass by without us pausing to recognise that they are a metaphor for what can be a life-changing moment breaking into the mundane of every day. We hesitate to call this a magic moment, but it is just that: a light shining in our difficult and dark places.

It is a small step from that point to realise how important the moment is. It is important for all of us to make the most of the moments, realising that life and death are always about moments. For me, music takes on high value for the most exciting and joyful events and for the times of great sadness and sorrow. In the deserts and the jungles, in cultures across the world, music is played and heard. It is deeply woven into our psychology and theology and yet widely ignored for the part it plays in mind and emotion, in solitude, and our largest celebrations.

AVOIDING STEREOTYPES

My moments and moods lead me to reflect that when I was in my late thirties, I had no conception of what it would be like to live such a long life. Four of my siblings have long since died. I did not think about what living to an old age might mean. I was too busy living. I am acutely aware that I am now living my last years.

In my consulting room, I meet many young men and women. In time, of course, they will become older men and women. An older man reflects tearfully on a time 66 years earlier, when as a ship's commander he gave orders to leave a raft carrying 20 or 30 young men, and they were swallowed up by the North Sea. An older woman remembers herself at nine years of age prevented from seeing her mother before she died, being introduced soon after to her stepmother, who knew how to destroy a child's self-worth because she had apparently suffered similar destruction of her self-worth. Another man was ready to live a retired life when he suffered a severely disabling stroke. His wife who never knew how to love a person, and his family certainly did not love him, was faced with the overwhelming conflict of complying with her children's wishes or expectations of looking after their father, though they had long since abandoned him after years of his aggressive domination and destructiveness.

In reflecting on these older people, notice that the first speaks of an event 66 years earlier. The second person's mother died 70 years ago. The husband of the third person suffered the stroke 18 years ago. Each one speaks of how they coped with an event, how that event affected them, how it changed their lives for decades afterwards, and what the event had come to mean for their view of themselves: self-pride, self-worth, self-efficacy, and self-confidence. Not all older men and women are resigned to the stereotypes of ageing. They report gathering in groups of ageing people, doing things that young people would not dream of doing, while others seem to have found their 'second wind' in their later years. Perhaps they realise they don't have much time left. Said a longstanding colleague of the same age, 'dying — what a waste! Why is my usefulness to society tied up with my chronological age?'

TOWARDS BETTER PSYCHOLOGICAL HEALTH

When I first entered psychology school, I was struck by what I thought was 'bad psychology'. It taught that the critical development years were in infancy and childhood. Early educational experiences, early milestones, early parental training would define who you would be in later life. Intelligence was some 'thing' you had or inherited. If you were lucky enough to have 'good' teachers, your growth pattern — even your intelligence — could be on an upward gradient until you reached early adulthood, then there was a static period — a plateau of ongoing experience. Those who did well in psychology aptitude tests of that time could be selected into careers not available to people who scored low points on those intelligence scales. A huge psychological travesty was committed as this plateau view of growth and achievement was widely accepted, and worse — vigorously taught.

A quiet revolution then began to take place. It revealed that the plateau idea was incorrect. People who had a poor early education could be lifted into a new stage of development. Development was a reality until people reached about 30 years of age and then it took a wide arc-like shape until decline began to set in, usually accepted as middle age, and the beginning of an inevitable decline.

A WORK IN PROGRESS

Not so long ago, it was widely accepted that with

the beginning of decline came an acceptance that growing old, or growing older, carried the expectation that people after 60 had a limited life ahead and they were often losing the ability to participate in a rapidly changing world. But a quiet realisation brought awareness that people were living 30 years longer than their parents and grandparents did. Discoveries in the fields of health and wellbeing found that living a good old age could happen. Not just because of 'good luck', but as a result of better health practices, better understanding of the psychology of ageing, better relationships, and better education and enjoyment.

The line of growth changed from the plateau to a stronger continuous upward gradient. Rather than accepting old age as an 'end point', it can be a work in progress, as people move through the identifiable stages of ageing. Some feared that with increased longevity, older people would be increasingly miserable. That has been the situation for many, and it will be so unless ageing can be done more intelligently, constructively, and enjoyably.

A NEW REALITY

We can approach our ageing as something that

happens, hopefully in good physical health. Or we can also approach ageing with intelligent strengths arising from an awareness of our psychological health. This involves us shaping our different identity as we age. We now pay much more attention to our physical health. What is needed is an increased understanding of the role of our psychological strengths.

Emotionally, ageing involves strengthening and expanding our positive emotions, finding harmony and engagement in our various relationships. Above all else, we need to develop a trajectory into the future, a future that we will live fully and well. The question is, of course, are we ready for it? Some fear what might happen, but give little precise thought to the important protections that they need as they run into the challenges and transitions of the vital years that remain to them.

As we live longer, we know that growing older involves adapting to the reality that life is not what it was. The future will be different from the past. There is a need to adapt to what has happened in the past; and there is a need to adapt to meet the unfolding circumstances of the future. There are people in their early old age who show a mild cognitive impairment, and begin to surrender to the belief that Alzheimer's disease will follow.

The reality is that progress to dementia may not occur. Some show a slow decline over many years. For others, decline may occur along with changes in their vascular health, sudden change in their social and living arrangements, and growing fears of their helplessness. Adaptation is about the past, and it is about finding the readiness and the resources to live constructively and enjoyably in and for the future. The task before them is to adapt to what has occurred, and adapt to what the future will bring. Shaping life for the future may involve adapting to a changed identity, reorganising financial resources, finding different social relationships, social engagements and social enjoyments.

REALITY CHECKING

Growing into our older years carries troublesome anxieties:

- How will I cope with old age?
- What provisions should I make for a time when I may not be able to care for myself?
- How can I attend to such matters when the future is unpredictable, and the onset of a critical need may be one or two decades away?

The good news is that there are social

predictors that can help make ageing a more comfortable time and provide some containment and control over the anxieties associated with old and very old age.

Although it is often said in passing that 'old age is creeping up on us', the more pressing reality is discovering that we are old. The signs are there — we stumble and almost fall; we realise that an occasional memory blip becomes a more common awareness; we lose our sense of direction; sleeping 'right through' is no longer a regular pattern, but light-sleeping and bladder discomfort become an all-too-common experience. We notice we are not standing up straight but are more and more attracted to the hunched position. Once we ran down the stairs, but a change occurs when someone says, 'you take the handrail'. Some lose interest in exercise, while others, with some anxiety, increase their activity.

It is the same with our social interests and other social enjoyments. Some say, 'it's normal', others say, 'he's starting to lose it'. There are those who age with aches and pains, and there are those who one day simply discover not only are they are getting old — they are old! The task is to be old intelligently, successfully, and enjoyably. And at the end of our days, when, as Scripture says, we take our allotted place, some will feel justified in saying 'we did it well'. Others might wonder if there was ample forgiveness for the mistakes they made.

The questions to be considered become many. Whether their life was very long or long enough, did they find sufficient harmony and gratitude so that the many fragments through the years found some themes of wholeness and acceptance, and that their life was enriching for more than simply themselves? Did they experience sufficient courage to transcend the deepest anguish and be enfolded into a caring quietness of life's ending, and 'peace at the last'?

MAKING THE NECESSARY TRANSITIONS

One of our greatest challenges is making the transition from work to retirement. The experience is often spoken of as if there is an anticipation that it will occur with some relief that work is over and a carefree enjoyable life is ahead. For some, that may be how it is, but most quickly realise there are many unforeseen events for which they have little preparation. There is the loss of professional identity, loss of purpose in life, loss of significant people and shared experiences. These arrive along with the challenges in finding new friendships, social belonging, and meaningful interests.

There is the increasing expectation that individuals will exercise responsibility for their health, their relationships, and their financial independence. Perhaps retirement was once 'brushed under the carpet' and regarded as a single expectation of everyone. Instead, we now recognise it as a complex social and psychological process that may take on very different forms from what we expected. And it may occur over an extended period of time.

My lawyer said his father, always a busy health professional, had looked forward to retirement when he would 'do the things he had always wanted to do'. But he developed health problems, which spread over three years and left him 'worn out' and no longer interested in making the necessary adaptations which took a further three years. Six years passed after he formally retired, and by that time friends and former colleagues had moved away from him. The positively anticipated retirement was now no longer a reality.

PLANNING OR STUMBLING

Prior to stopping work, many people try to imagine

what they will 'do'. But frequently the realities bear little resemblance to their imagined retirement. Some avoid imagining their retirement, and some health or family factor may force the decision to retire at a time when they are unprepared for it. Both men and women talk about their imagined retirement, but do little to prepare for it. Studies have shown that while planning can be an important predictor of subsequent health, that planning may not predict retirement satisfaction.

When we experience a decline in our self-image and self-worth we become less interested in responsible planning for our older years. Some were so busy at work that they had not recognised that they would be made redundant. From being a strong worker, committed to the goals of the company, they became someone who 'had to be let go'. Where redundancy has been the key factor in retirement, it may affect the timing of a planned retirement, and have a major impact on the sense of self worth and social status. It can precipitate a prolonged period of disillusionment and suppressed rage which interferes with their thinking of how to organise retirement and effectively adapt to the changes involved.

When we are 55, a plan for living to 85 and

beyond seems irrelevant. Usually, we just 'hope' things will somehow sort themselves out. We do not see the point of considering that the next 30 years will have events that we could not predict and that might be loaded with realities for which we could not prepare. Some aspects of physical and mental deterioration can be prevented through exercise, or softened through specific forms of social support and emotional stimulation. But other events, such as a major accident or illness, can occur without any warning.

We find that a plan for living may only become consciously relevant after something has occurred — after a serious injury, after a diagnosis of a life-threatening illness, after the loss of a relationship, after the collapse of self-confidence. Is a plan a realistic possibility, or do most people 'take life as it comes' or 'somehow get by' without formulating a plan? Does it matter?

A plan may provide a purpose — a purpose to put into effect the plan. Many plans are little more than daydreams or fantasies, vague hopes, or even a pathway along which considerable time and energy are engaged — a sense of purpose. What are the possibilities? What possibility can become part of the formulation of a plan and give rise to a sense of purpose? A purpose may mean participating in the large picture or it may be a multifaceted activity that can bring an experience of pleasure, or even of passion.

A person's purpose may be their commitment to become a member of the orchestra. That will require a plan to develop a particular musical competence. That person may explore various possibilities, and then develop the smaller purposes that will serve the larger purpose. Although this process may at times be 'painful', one larger purpose is to uncover various layers of pleasure — instrumental competence, recognition of status and position in the orchestra, the quality of music produced, the acceptance and acclamation of audiences, the interpersonal and group enjoyments, life satisfaction, financial gain and security, a fantasy of the future.

THE FOUR PS – PLAN, PURPOSE, POSSIBILITIES, PLEASURE

As we age we experience many subjective and social pressures to recognise and pursue the four Ps (plan, purpose, possibilities, pleasure) but we frequently find that they do not come easily, and are not readily sustained. Recognising that we need a plan, a purpose, possibilities, and the enjoyment of pleasures, is not enough. What is needed is how we go about it. The exhortation to take up a hobby, to sustain an involvement in sport, to call up a few friends, to go on a cruise, may ultimately become unsustainable.

At many points along the way we hit a 'stale-mate'. We find ourselves settling for full-time television punctuated by prolonged daytime dozing or sleeplessness at night. We become conflicted between passivity and participation, between deterioration and depression, between interests and inspiration, between flatness and enjoyment, between neurotic withdrawal and frantic or needy involvements. It can be such an unpredictable experience. When we believe we have found an accepted level of enjoyment, reading the daily death notices reminds us of the sadness and suffering that have come to many who had expected pleasure but were confronted with emotional and physical pain.

Focusing on A Process

1. A revision of the past and release from its painful aspects.
2. A redefinition of the self and expectations

regarding the future.

3. Greater authenticity in relationships.
4. Clarity of goals and commitments.
5. Adaptation to the unfolding realities.
6. Reaching a sense of satisfaction and gratitude.
7. A resolution of life's completion.
8. Relinquishing life to the next generation.

TRAINING THE BRAIN

The neuroscientists tell us the brain is not wired for happiness, but it is wired to learn. Some have found that no matter what their experiences, it is possible to grow and learn through them. Yet when we come to discuss brain health, brain capacity, or brain performance, some older people are ready to give themselves a 'fail'. They learnt that readiness when they were 10 years old: can't add-up, can't remember their multiplication tables after weeks of trying, can't remember if a particular word has two c's or two m's or one c and one m. The nightmare of childhood classes may suddenly crash into their older years. We can become convinced that we are 'losing' our mind.

We realise we can't remember Harry and Jill, we make a mess of checking how much money we have after the supermarket purchases, and become convinced that we have a disease and can't stop our mind going over the symptoms again and again. When we were younger, we used to fall asleep 'anywhere'. In our older years, our brain is so active that we can't get off to sleep — for 'the fourth time this week!' Many people do the daily crossword, follow several mind exercises, concealing the fear that failing to do these exercises will hasten the onset of Alzheimer's disease, or will prove that they are in a comprehensive cognitive decline.

STRESSES AND CHALLENGES

As we age we face different stresses and challenges from the younger person. The older person has no particular need to perform speed-and-accuracy tests, or to remember how to spell 'ornithorhynchus'. They may never have the need to do that subtraction of starting at 200 and subtracting over and over at high speed. But they may have discovered they can relax (as they never could when younger) and enjoy exquisite music. They may realise they have the patience and emotional readiness to learn to play the piano or oboe.

The ageing brain may be different from the impatient youthful brain. It may open areas of contentment and inspiration that were never considered by the younger brain. It is a surprise to many carers to discover that an ageing person experiences deterioration and yet an emotional awareness indicating that some aspects of brain functioning are better than in younger years. An aged person may appear to have little response to the passing events of the day, but will respond with appropriate emotional warmth to the sight of a baby or the presence of the family dog. Many of our cognitive functions may have deteriorated beyond retrieval, but the emotional brain functioning may be accessible and accurately intact.

We tend to take our mind for granted until it does not function as it once did. The mind leaves us worrying over trivial things. The mind distorts some good experiences into misery. Our mind can rush us into confusion and worry, but it can take us into the most beautiful experiences. Some people serve the world in life-saving ways by training their minds to perform the most intricate tasks — as in microsurgery or in playing tennis at a high level of skill.

GAINING EMOTIONAL INTELLIGENCE

During childhood and through adolescence to young adulthood, the acquisition of cognitive skills was a high priority. People preparing for employment, and to take on a productive role in its institutions, needed to develop certain skills. Their suitability for specific careers and occupations could be aligned with their cognitive versatility. Little was done to track or evaluate their emotional and relationship skills or the importance for their employment in society and to the maintenance of their health and well-being.

The intelligence needed in early years is no longer as relevant when we age. Intelligence in older years involves a concern for what skills and resources are required for the years of retirement, transition and change. This will include adaptation to many changes, finding satisfaction and enjoyment in relationships, emotional stimulation and inspiration, careful thinking for the final years of life, and the quality of life in those years.

Some people decide to 'just let it happen'. Many will recognise that the final years can be boring and empty. These years can be intelligently, successfully, and enjoyably lived as they integrate the past into the present, as they resolve to relinquish their need to 'settle everything', and enter the spiritual integrity of their life-course. Whereas educational institutions have been active in preparing people for life in their earlier and middle years, the institutions of the spirit have been largely irrelevant in providing resources for these later years of integrity and fulfilment.

Our mind can be developed to be engaged in very specialised activities or to do routine rote tasks every day, or it can deteriorate and become unpredictable and uncontrollable. Many discover that this highly valuable 'control station' can lose many of its functions that provide us with our identity, direction, and belonging, including our mental functioning and mental health. It is such a vital part of our life, but we know so little about it, and we are largely unaware of how to preserve our mind in good health.

The same applies to our ability to manage our memories. There are unhappy memories that dominate our day. The task is to practise filtering out toxic memories and filter in good memories. Good memories enhance identity and remind us of good places and good people. Good memories bring a sense of enjoyment and enlargement to existence. They are also able to bring a sense of who we 'were' and who we 'are'.

Frequently you will hear people say, 'That does not make sense'. Life has lost its meaning. The task is to re-find meaning in your life. Without that sense of meaning and purpose you are vulnerable to depression, disgruntlement, and disillusionment. For some, meaning and purpose come easily — perhaps their family relationships spontaneously explode with events that give life its positive meaning. For others, it is difficult to find a satisfactory meaning in anything. Most people come to realise that meaning does not 'just happen'. They have to give meaning to a difficult experience. They might have to impose meaning on a meaningless event. The phases of emotional intelligence follow:

Phases of Emotional Intelligence

1. The phase of identity transition — the person moves out of employment to retirement, out of a designated occupation to a time of discovering who and what they will be.
2. Cultural adaptation — the person searches for resources to adapt to their changing culture (e.g. from the work culture to the retirement culture).
3. Enhanced reappraisal — the person reviews the life course, the years that may be ahead of them, the resources available to them — the wider embrace of possibilities of activity and fulfilment.

4. Interpretation of what have been important values, experiences and relationships. This could also include ways other people, institutions and spiritual resources have enriched our life, and how we might have enriched them in return.

MAINTAINING EMOTIONAL HEALTH

Our emotional health is first of all about emotions. Emotional health is vitally concerned with a person's self-worth, self-confidence and self-enjoyment. It is also vitally concerned with interpersonal acceptance and confirmation, with interpersonal affability and collaboration. Where conflict and disharmony occur, the level of emotional health plays a large part in how effectively the distress can be contained and corrected to reach a constructive resolution.

Maintaining our emotional health as we age involves the comfortable and successful management of anger and resentments, attractions and attachments, bereavements and grief, investments in memories, and loss of, or damage to, emotional investments. In a broad sense, emotional health is manifested in the individual, between other people, between significant others, with family members, and in the world. It is contextual, involving past events and perceptions of them, and the further projections and fantasies about the past and future.

It could be argued that older people having lived longer, have had more experience with emotional discomfort and conflict, and should be able to cope with them more effectively. But people hold onto grievances, even when it would be wiser to let them go. At one level, people want their hurts to be soothed, but at another level, they resist the soothing they would like to have. Having been hurt, some may reject necessary healing; strong convictions and attitudes about the issue are confirmed by retelling the story about the injustice or the wrong that was done.

Contributors to Positive Emotional Health

1. Events and experiences that encourage and evoke the emotions of enjoyment, contentment and excitement.
2. Experiences that foster a sense of identity and belonging. There is a widely held expectation that a family belonging is given high rating, often without adequate recognition of the frustrations and resentments that are frequently concealed in family relationships. Hostility and negative memories can be more binding than love and enjoyable memories.

3. Relationships that provide stability and support, caring and compassion, interest and inspiration.
4. Experiences of love, work, and play, social engagement and expansiveness of the human spirit through art and music, relaxation and meditation, spiritual awareness and a religious belonging.
5. Finding an interest, a purpose, a cause that will give a sense of meaning and value to one's existence.
6. Developing ways to establish an inner harmony, transcending negative emotional states and proactively creating positive life-enhancing environments.

We know that the strengths of younger years may not be the strength we need to cope more effectively as we age. A psychology of ageing provides some practical guidelines. We have rarely been taught how to soften painful memories, how to get free of relationship hurts, how to get some release from painful events of the past. Some have difficulty getting over their losses; others find their last years heavy going. Peace of mind can be lost as we worry, as we become overwhelmed by discontent and disillusionment. Some rely on a backup of personality strengths but these can be crowded out by a loss of confidence and loss of coping skills. These years bring with them unique and difficult challenges. If we are to live them better, more effectively and more enjoyably, some preparation is needed.

Sigmund Freud drew attention to our defense mechanisms — so important for the management of our anxieties. To these I add our release mechanisms — the processes that 'release' us from persisting resentments, release us from distressing memories, release us from destructive relationships.

Release Processes

1. Recognise that the distressing 'bad' experience event, memory, person or institution can be identified as external objects, and also experienced as internal objects. Both are distressing. We need release from both.
2. Reposition the self in relation to the external object — move away from it / fence it off.
3. Drain the negative energy that has become invested in an external and inner object. Decrease the investment; diminish the size or power of the inner object.
4. This process usually requires an alliance with

a professional person to guide and sustain the process, and to strengthen, soothe and reconstruct self-worth and self-image.

5. Restrengthen the resistance to relapsing into negative, self-punitive, and self-diminishing impulses.
6. Re-establish a fantasy of the future, and continually focus on its positive attributes and strengths.
7. Constantly arrest the compulsion to relapse and repeat the past distress, and the tendency to hold onto the trauma that is past.
8. Study and learn internal self-soothing processes, including meaningful activities and experiences that provide pleasure.

Above, I have highlighted the need to be aware of the pathology and challenges of ageing. Many long lasting problems in old age can be prevented. Some can be soothed and softened. In the next chapter, I will explore ways to prevent some of these problems, and to restrengthen our emotionally fragile places, and how our ageing might be done more successfully and enjoyably.

Chapter 2

Thriving Not Surviving

As we live longer, growing older has many hazards. Somehow we, the average elderly, cope, even with terrible disasters. The goal is ever before us: how to adapt in our ageing years, how to rise above serious difficulties, how to live through our declining years, and still age successfully, enjoyably, generously. To address these vitally important issues, for almost forty years, I conducted groups for older adults, their age ranging between 55-100 years. We called these groups SAGE groups — Successful Ageing with Growth and Enhancement — claiming it was a sensible wisdom to learn how to adapt to the losses in growing old. In recent years, I have changed the name of these groups to AWE — 'Ageing With Expectation'. These groups consistently attract 80–100 people, wanting to be part of a 'life-long learning' experience.

These groups involve identifying and learning the vital protective factors that would lessen the common troubles of ageing. We identified uncontrolled worry, loss of confidence, depression in its various forms, loss of control over our lives and our emotions. The question hit us — are we destined to an inevitable decline as we age, or can we become active in slowing that decline? Our objective was learning more about the psychology of ageing, identifying individual strengths and sourcing community resources. Our aim was to ensure we stay 'alive' until we die. We identified many factors that help keep our vitality, our optimism, and our sense of worth.

PERSONALITY FACTORS

Personality is a word most often used to describe our way of being in the world: he is a very likeable person; she is very argumentative. Such descriptions refer to personality traits and tendencies, personality development and dispositions. Our personality consists of the thoughts, feelings and behaviour, the attitudes beliefs and lifestyle that we bring to the world, and through which we respond to the circumstances, challenges and traumas in the different stages of the lifespan. At one point the concern of educators and researchers focused on personality factors or expressions that were seen to contribute to social adjustment and success. In older age, the focus moved to a concern with personal resilience and the cognitive, emotional, and relationship factors that contribute to lifespan health and adaptation and enjoyment.

In our earlier years most of us were aware of the strengths in our personality, how we fitted in socially, and explored limits of our mental and cognitive functioning. As we grew older, a diminished view of our personality became a major personal and social concern. At a personal level, we became anxious about what kind of person we had become, whether we had fulfilled the dream of what would be possible. At a social level, there was concern about our social interaction, social enjoyment and social happiness in specific groups and in society more generally.

Another factor is to recognise how our

executive functions decline as we age. These functions include driving a vehicle, household duties, management of finances, and maintaining independence in daily life. It is recognised that decline in one or more areas of executive functioning will likely have consequences for our everyday activities. In the past, such decline was considered generalised, but now with more specific analysis it is possible to identify which functions are affected, what can reduce the decline, and what compensatory and protective processes may be involved.

AGEING INTELLIGENTLY

In our SAGE and AWE groups we discovered a 'new age' was not as far away as we first expected. We found a new ageing intelligence, an ageing wisdom that opened us to a more successful and enjoyable stage of life. Ageing intelligently could save a lot of worry. It could help us to live much longer and more successfully. It could replace the fear, and the waste of our older years. It could point us to something better than the 'inevitabilities' we have hitherto accepted. In other words, a more informed and intelligent ageing changes the way we age.

We know there are many manifestations of intelligence. We learned in our school days that intelligence determined who we were and what we might become. Tests were developed to measure it and on the basis of an allocated score, a person's future life trajectory would be proposed. One person had intelligence that would take them into a high career; another had intelligence that placed them in a lower social level of basic manual labour.

We know that in addition to this so-called 'cognitive' intelligence, there are other intelligences: social intelligence, emotional intelligence, sporting intelligence, ageing intelligence, spiritual intelligence. Ageing intelligence embraces capacities of adaptation to old age, old age losses and gains, social interests and social engagements and social enjoyment. Some people are low on ageing adaptation and adapting to old age, adapting to the changes that are part of moving through the stages of aging, stages of growth and stagnation, of social wisdom and social emptiness of relationship expansiveness and relationship impoverishment. Exposed to different pathways of growth, patterns of living, environments and influences, some people will demonstrate high levels of ageing intelligence.

Others may show little interest in sustaining their ageing intelligence.

STAGES OF INTELLIGENT AGEING

Emotional Vitality

In our late fifties and sixties, the first stage involves the anticipation of sustaining emotional vitality and an active enjoyable social interest. Although they recognise the losses that are beginning to occur (loss of some functioning, loss in relationships, loss in status), there is a growth in anticipation of changes ahead — changes in family life, occupational, in social relationships, in personal and social enjoyments. This anticipation may have loadings of enjoyment and anxiety, of vitality and hope.

Adaptation

As individuals enter their late sixties, they begin to recognise that they need to relinquish several aspects of their life. This stage involves further adaptation. They will relinquish some dreams, they will relinquish some relationships, and they will relinquish the position and status they once held. They will relinquish life goals that were once important to them. This will centre around anxiety in different aspects of life and the vital task will be finding ways to contain this anxiety for this stage of life to be managed successfully.

Reshaping

As they approach their seventieth year, men and women will have seen the need or been required to reshape their lives. Certain experiences bring many changes. Loss, grief and relationship changes require reshaping of goals, and sources of energy and enjoyment. In their eighties, there is a repositioning of meaning and purpose, of passion and pleasure. People in this stage realise that they are in the last two decades of their existence. Achievements and enjoyments take on different meanings. Physical conditions may bring limitations to activities and this will involve reshaping of expectations in the light of prevailing realities.

Repositioning

Emotional sensitivities may become more pressing than at earlier times. Resentments and irritabilities may begin to crowd the interpersonal discourse. This stage requires a repositioning of the self in relation to these stresses and the resources that will be needed to cope consistently with them.

A different arrangement of life and its space will be necessary. There may be a strong tendency to deny, evade, or avoid the pleasures and passions of this stage. Deliberate action will be necessary to reposition these passions and pleasures as valid parts of successful ageing. Repositioning will mean arranging the place and people to allow a positive flow of pleasure and passion.

Accepting

The fourth stage involves a sense of relief at passing through their final years without the signs of unmanageable decline or without the onset of illness and disease. It can become the time of resolving to meet decline and death with acceptance and gratitude. Some have experienced difficult burdens of pain and disablement over several decades, and at times their ambivalence over death may become a strong desire that death might bring the relief that seems so much more preferable to their chronic physical and mental pain. But the hope persists that the end of life will be experienced as peaceful.

ESTABLISHING PURPOSE AND FINDING MEANING

Two of the most important tasks confronting us as we age is establishing purpose and finding meaning. The task in front of us includes maintaining positive moods and emotions. These are influenced by many factors, by past learning, by experience, by the strengths of social confirmation and support, and by the accumulation of optimistic expectations. A further task is to maintain life satisfactions, recognising that this is a protection against a decline in health, an opening to the engagement in adaptive behaviours, and increasing the likelihood of longevity.

Some younger people have no specific purpose in life; they get on with the smaller purposes in life, finding and keeping a job, getting good results in their examinations, finding and keeping some good friends, staying healthy. Older people who come to realise that they have lost their purpose in life might say, 'There has to be more in life than spending three hours reading the daily newspaper when you bought it only to read the obituaries' or 'There must be more to life than watching the same television program every night'.

How will we sustain a positive purpose in life?

How do we develop a purpose in life when we recognise that we have lost it? Is it important to have a purpose in life, and what form will it need to take? Having a satisfying purpose in life is like catching the right train. Many people discover they are on the wrong emotional, relational, social, and career train. At a critical moment when they would value some help to get onto the right train, they find there are few people willing or able to help them. Some of them will get off the train and sit waiting for the right train to come. They find that waiting can be boring and sometimes dangerous.

Many will tell of their experiences, of the trains they have missed, the trains they should have taken, and of the trains that will never come. A purpose in life provided them with a reason to live each day. It kept them alive and hopeful. It made them socially interesting and socially productive. They may have been in productive employment until they reached retirement, only to realise that the purposes that had solidly sustained enjoyment, satisfaction, and a sense of well being, have all disappeared. Many turn to sporting activities, hobbies, social clubs, and a spread of friendships to avoid feelings of loneliness, boredom and relationship emptiness. For others, the only purpose they have is the persisting quarrel with their husband, wife, a family member, or some past friend or business partner.

Yet there is strong acceptance of the experience and belief that a purpose in life contributes to life's enjoyment and vitality. A purpose in life is likely to increase positive emotions of happiness, life satisfaction, and overall wellbeing. How is it sustained over different phases of the lifespan, and in the face of stressful events that undermine it? If it is relevant and meaningful for people of all ages and particularly in old age, what do we need to do that is different, what form will it take, and what experiences will need to be activated to sustain it?

Purpose in Life Factors in Middle Years

- Significant relationships.
- Satisfying and challenging goals and aspirations.
- Commitment to a meaningful activity, work goals and achievements.
- Influences on self-worth and personal affirmations.
- Inspirational stories, models, people in the present, past and future.

- Hobbies, social and sporting interests and engagements.
- Political awareness, belonging and engagement.

Purpose in Life Factors in Old Age

- Sustaining social and community relationships.
- Attention to home maintenance.
- Care of the family pet.
- Planning the summer holiday.
- Maintaining physical fitness.
- Family activities.

ACQUIRING EMOTIONAL RESILIENCE

A basic task to ageing successfully is to become aware of the factors that contribute to emotional resilience and enjoyment. As we age there is a recurring difficulty in finding and sustaining a focus. One reason is that high levels of frustration may exist when people feel they cannot attain a satisfying life purpose, or they cannot reach an integrative point where there is an acceptance of life and its meaning. Individuals who cannot do so tend to lead an unfocused life, with various levels of boredom, discontent and depression.

By contrast, a number of older adults

develop a spontaneous purpose in living which gives them, and their significant others, energy, vitality and a strong goal direction. We notice they take appropriate steps to maintain their appearance, they maintain social interests and social engagements, and a sense of participation in a community and its causes. Neglecting these basic tasks means we may lose perspective on life's challenges, or may slide into isolation and loneliness, despondency and depression.

DEVELOPING EMOTIONAL RESILIENCE

Loneliness is experienced in the context of other people, the context of a particular community, or the context of a specific activity. It may be a generalised experience that affects one's general adaptation to, and enjoyment of, life. While some report that they 'never' feel lonely, that they can't remember the 'last time' they felt lonely, others will need constant reminders that they are liked and loved, and that they are constantly supported and assured in their attachment and belonging to certain groups. Loneliness has an impact on our social interaction and enjoyment, and a sense of social competence, our self-worth, and emotional and mental health.

Although women have stronger social-talking groups and support groups than men, they are likely to report feeling lonely more often than men. Becoming a widow, living alone, a low self-concept, absence of an engaging purpose, or pleasure, low socio-economic status, ill health, physical disability, anxiety and depression, are persisting challenges. We also know that men are reluctant to admit to loneliness, and they are widely reported to have fewer friends than women. Some rely heavily on their marriage and family even when the level of interaction and enjoyment is low. It is clear the absence of emotional loneliness increases our resilience and sustains optimism and hopefulness about our life and our role in it. A number of emotional strengths contribute to resilience or our ability to 'bounce back' and try again:

Emotional Strengths and Resilience

1. Strengths to accept that some things will not change.
2. Strengths to 'let go' and refocus life directions.
3. Strengths to turn adversity to some advantage.
4. Strengths to remain quiet when anxiety is at a high level.
5. Strengths to accept other people without being overcome by their demands.

6. Strengths to accept the reality of contradictions.
7. Strengths to stay focused on the best goals and outcomes.

ADAPTING AND CELEBRATING

The big task facing everyone is to adapt to the realities of life. The requirements of adaptation may change at different points across the life span, facing different stresses, changing levels of resources and changing awareness of those resources and access to them. Our human species is constantly involved in adapting to its physical, social and interpersonal environments. The focus here is an adaptation to the various losses that impinge on every individual: the death of a valued or significant other; failure to achieve a valued objective; the loss of one's coping capacities and valued supports.

Another major consideration in adapting is finding purpose and meaning — life did not 'turn out' the way we would have hoped. How do we cope with the outcome: How do we adapt to the reality that is in front of us? A catastrophe occurs. A disappointment disrupts a planned holiday and many people will be affected. An accident requires hospitalisation of several weeks. A marriage of 30 years is terminated. The list of adverse events accumulates in our memory.

There are many pleasant events that also require acceptance and adaptation. A person wins the lottery. Your spouse receives a high career appointment that will require relocating to another country. You have survived two heart attacks. You are about to be married again. You have just taken delivery of a pet dog. You have received news that could be life changing. All of these will become part of adapting to a new reality and discovering the resources that will be relevant to that reality. The range of reactions may include joy and happiness, or involve conflict, anxiety and guilt.

EXPANSIVE AGEING – LIVING TO 100

People tell me 'I don't want to live to a hundred'. I will ask them 'how long do you want to live?' They might continue by disclosing their anxiety about being very old — 'You see those pictures of old people having their hundredth birthday. They look so frail. They are just skin and bone'. Who wants to live to 100 if it means increasing dependence, loss of several physical capacities, and an uncertainty regarding the reliability of memory and enjoyment?

Supposing the conditions of life changed — and people were given the capacity to live 100 years. Everyone. Would they live it differently? What would occur if everyone, not given a guarantee of a hundred years, nevertheless were educated from early childhood to plan to live to 100? Would they live differently? Would they make plans to avoid some dangerous experiences and damaging places? What will contribute to their healthy successful old age? What will be the predictors and protectors?

While the response of many will be the hope of sustaining their physical health, perhaps few would see that having a purpose in life would be also as important. They may readily identify their various physical losses of old age, but may not recognise how their psychological resources and attributes may be both protective and predictive of a satisfying and successful old age. One critical factor is how they adapt to the losses, changes, demands and uncertainties and what resources they will bring to this adaptational challenge. If adaptation is low, there is likely to be considerable discontent. Very old people find their social networks will have diminished, and intimacy satisfactions are likely to fall away.

ONE DAY AT A TIME

I have heard many claim, 'We will just take it as it comes', 'We'll live one day at a time'. Others will be aware that there are some things that should be avoided, like excessive exercise, drinking, smoking, accidents and a range of risky behaviours. But better health, and some rational planning, may mean our later years can be a pleasure for our own life and for the lives of those who are close to us. Some people develop lifestyles and conditions that mean their life will be over as soon as they hit 70 and thus entertaining thoughts of living another thirty years are unrealistic. Others will find they have reached old age without any plan as it just happened. Could they have done the last 25 years better, more enjoyably, with a greater sense of satisfaction and fulfilment?

There is an observable tendency for people in their 90s to become more enclosed, claiming to be 'happy' as the larger part of their days are spent sleeping and eating, staring into space, waiting for someone to visit. What is appropriate behaviour for a person 96 years of age? Need we accept that such people in their old age will decline into dementia? Even if this is the case, what considered pleasures and satisfactions are available to them? Many believe that inactivity and passivity are fully acceptable — that it is a great relief to be free of the demands, expectations, and anxieties of earlier years. Others will argue that by rational transitions, they can continue to draw satisfactions and enjoyments into a lifestyle in which the decade of 95–105 will be regarded as a successful way of ageing. What might we look for — and aim for — in this decade of advanced ageing?

What to Look For

1. An awareness of some softness and soothing experiences for past and present pains. Look for times and places of quietness and healing.
2. An openness to live with a positive attitude, positive emotions, good humour and a quiet appreciation, expressive enjoyments.
3. Alternative ways of coping with the anxieties of everyday life.
4. Maintaining a 'vital spark', a positive fantasy about the past and the future, looking back with pleasure, looking forward with anticipation.
5. Selecting meaningful enjoyable experiences with the world and with some specific people — social interest, social participation, social enjoyment and social sympathy.

6. Holding a strong sense of identify and self-worth in spite of difficulties and decline.
7. A sense of spiritual belonging, spiritual strength and protections.
8. A sense of spiritual belonging within a physical and interpersonal context.
9. Where dementia and disabilities are the dominant factors, there is a rational need for appropriate care in a safe holding environment.

What to Avoid

1. As far as possible, avoid illness, disease and injury.
2. As far as possible, avoid unpleasant memories, avoid anxieties that run out of control; avoid fears of what might happen in the future.
3. Avoid angry negative people, negative emotions, and negative moods.
4. Avoid adopting old age stereotypes.
5. Avoid ruminating on past achievements, past mistakes, past hurts.
6. Avoid slipping into untidiness in dress, mode of speech, and daily habits.

MAKING THE RIGHT CHOICES

Most of us accept that we may not live to be 100. We may not wish to be one of a few surviving centenarians. But do they want their lives to end before they have run their full course? Or do they accept there is nothing they can do about it, and so they wait until their life comes to its 'natural end'? But what is that natural end? Do we expect life to peter-out quietly, or do we fear the end we so often see, where the very old are burdened with daily aches and pains, prolonged illnesses requiring prolonged treatment?

What then will make very old age an attractive goal? If we took a busload of fifty 60 year olds (male and female) on a learning camp to teach them the qualities and resources they will need to live to 100 and more, what would be the high priorities in the learning program? We immediately have some difficulties. First the number of people currently living to 100 is small and most are inaccessible as a group, and thus there would be limitations in asking what were the key factors that most contributed to their old age.

Secondly, popular enquiries made of centenarians regarding their long life yield usually superficial responses — 'I never touched alcohol', 'I stayed out of trouble', 'I suppose I was one of the lucky ones', 'I had many sickness as a child, but in my old age I just kept going', 'I never married'.

Thirdly, many of these long livers doubt if they will live to 100. No family member has done so. The people who had been their social networks had died years earlier. They see that they have two special characteristics that would lead them to believe they should live to 100.

Fourthly, the very old have been largely neglected in studies on ageing, the main concern has been to ensure their physical needs were cared for and they were kept interested in life around them.

MAJOR TASKS FOR THE WOULD-BE CENTENARIANS

If we ask a 20-year-old about their prospects of living to100, they would probably regard the question as too far removed from the current realities. If we ask a 60- or 70-year-old the same question, they might likely reply out of apprehension and fear. 'I don't want to be too long in God's waiting room'. They are quick to change the conversation. With better health information, lifestyle education, and the increase in caring facilities and general social interest, people are living into very old age.

There will be more centenarians.

In addition to coping with life's daily exigencies, centenarians will need to prepare to cope with losses and deteriorations, agility and mobility, loss of valued functions — sight, hearing, physical and dental health, decline in social interest and social support. They may struggle to find purposes in life, a worthwhile sustainable passion, a person to share enjoyments, an effective way to maintain self worth. They must cope not only with their current realities, but will need to create enjoyments and experience enhancements of life when the tendency may be to shift into inactivity and apathy.

A major task is to develop and sustain protections against rapid deterioration, the loss of supportive relationships and the slide into negativity, helplessness and depression as well as the acute and chronic diseases of late old age. Further tasks involve maintaining a purpose in life, keeping in touch with positive healing emotions, controlling anxieties and remaining focused in the necessary functions of life, fully able to be in control of one's life. Here are some of the factors that increase life satisfactions and contentment:

Life Satisfactions and Contentment

1. Freedom from physical illness and pain.
2. Freedom from anxiety and stress, health and economic worries, social expectations.
3. Positive relationships with family and others.
4. Sources of help and assistance for:
   - Basic purchases.
   - Basic care.
   - Basic accommodation and transportation.
5. Intelligent relevant enjoyable events, experiences.
6. Effective management of emotions and past experiences.
7. Beliefs about self — self confidence, self esteem, self content.
8. Capacities, attitudes, intentions to adapt to change, adapt to loss, adapt to the last phases of life.
9. A realistic ownership of the future, many aspects of which will be different from the past.

THE GREAT BEYOND

Where is 'The Great Beyond'? With better diet, better exercise, better medical and surgical knowledge, more rationality of mind, greater awareness of emotional and relationship satisfaction, a more open exploration of the spiritual aspects of personality and adaptation, we should realistically expect to live much longer. But negative and limited destinies have been inculcated into lifestyle expectancies so that we abandon the study of the psychology of life beyond 90.

Who lives in 'The Great Beyond'? We know that diseases and injuries can cut short a life of a person in their 20s or 40s. We see pictures of people celebrating their 105th birthday. They speak as if they have lost their vitality and vigour and all claims on life. They are hanging on. But they do not have any guarantee of a long and substantial survival. Instead of adopting an attitude of resignation to being old and frail, a more positive attitude could be adopted and a 'positive strengthening' the prevailing goal. Expansive ageing advocates a more determined forward ageing and has one or more of the following characteristics:

Expansive Ageing

1. Embrace the life of each day as a gift.
2. Explore positive ageing appropriate to the 90s and 100s through:
   - Reactive activity, e.g. the arts.
   - Challenged activity, e.g. 'do not go gently into that 'good night'.'
   - Interactive activity, e.g. within enjoyable relationships.
   - Regenerative activity, e.g. sport, relaxation, mindfulness, spirituality.
3. Plan to live to 100 and have a plan to do so.
4. Maintain a social interest, ageing education, ageing enjoyments, ecological participation.
5. Recognise stress, aim to prevent and to cope.
6. Practise the quietening of the mind.

THE CHALLENGES AND ANXIETIES OF INTELLIGENT AGEING

Growing into older years has its challenges and its anxieties. I have heard people ask what provisions should I make for a time when I cannot care for myself? How will I cope when I am on my own? These are important issues, given the future is unpredictable, and it may be two decades away before we need to make such decisions. The good news is that there are predictors that can help to make ageing a more comfortable time and provide some containment and control over these anxieties.

Growing older intelligently involves adapting to the reality that life is not what it was, and that the future will be different from the past. There is a need to adapt to what has happened in the past, just as there is a need to adapt to meet the unfolding circumstances of the future. The challenge is about finding the readiness and the resources to live constructively and enjoyably in the moment, and for the future. In effect, adaptation is adapting backwards and forwards. It involves adapting to a changed identity, reorganising financial resources, finding different social relationships, social engagements, and social enjoyments.

MAINTAINING SELF WORTH

Many are surprised how quickly families are too busy to spend time with elderly parents and friends. Older people are perceived as having less value than young people. Older people themselves say they feel brushed aside, and of less importance. A major task of ageing is to find ways to maintain self-worth and sustain self-compassion. This is an important task, as it is well known that a good sense of self-worth has positive benefits whatever our stage in life.

But self-worth is elusive and can often be difficult to maintain. We might find ourselves oscillating between two emotional poles. We might overplay our self-worth, self-confidence and self-compassion, often by asserting, or reminding ourselves of our achievements, good experiences and good memories. The other is a strong tendency to lose confidence in our capabilities, to succumb to the belief that we are no longer the person we once were, to accept we are past our 'use-by' date, and that we have lost our sense of worth in the world and our value to society. Places where we once felt valued as people of worth and held in high regard can become places that no longer listen to us, and become places of rejection or places of prejudice and pity.

AFFIRMATIONS AND ANXIETIES

In our younger years we are encouraged to believe that the world is our oyster, that with the development of inner strengths and competencies we can be in control of desired outcomes of happiness and success. In our older years, there is a strong tendency to believe that happiness and success are dependent on factors outside our control, like fate, destiny and chance. Thus, while a great effort is made to develop and maintain inner control over this ageing decline, there is a persisting strong belief that decline is inevitably controlled by external factors. The task of older people is to accept the reality of these external factors, but develop internal strengths to slow down and control them, and plan compensations where necessary.

There is a persisting anxiety that inner controls may diminish with ageing, and external control beliefs will increase. Loss of, or decrease in control beliefs will affect the person's morale and motivation, interpersonal pleasures and anxiety, their health and mortality. A major concern is how to maintain adequate internal control beliefs and how to decrease the external control beliefs so that there is an appropriate acceptance of the place of each.

As we begin to age, we become acutely conscious of our personal history, personal achievements, and personal aspirations and anxieties. In contemporary society, work provides a functional identity which provides an income which then opens up other identities that might define them as the owner of a luxury car, the occupant of a large villa in Italy, the owner of a family home in an Australian country town. These identities provide the sense of 'this is who I am, and this is the person I want to be'.

One question posed when we no longer wish to work, have been made redundant, or cannot work is, 'What are you going to do?' In childhood and youth a common question is 'What are you going to be?' — meaning what career will you pursue or what kind of job will be likely to suit your interests and capacities. In the early phase of retirement, 'being' is seen to be less important than the 'doing'. You need to find some interest, become part of some group, or develop some hobby — all in the context of doing something — something interesting? Something useful? Something enjoyable? Something to keep you active and alive?

You may not have articulated a rational or specific purpose in your early years. In your later years there is a heightened awareness that the purpose you once had is no longer relevant. If you were a nurse, schoolteacher, doctor, or carpenter, purposes unfolded within the interpretations and manifestations of the job or profession you once had. As you leave the paid workplace, its purposes that gave meaning and energy and focus to life, begin to disappear. Is it surprising that after a busy life spread over forty or sixty years, others become interested in or wonder what you will do, now that you have 'nothing to do'. Each day begins with the question, 'What are your plans for today?'

Life becomes more interesting and more liveable if you have an interest, even better if it is a passion. It may be an art class, a regular dancing engagement, it may be teaching an old dog new tricks, or it may be an occasional excitement derived from a win by your favourite sporting team. Many are satisfied if they can find a good place to be, a quiet, beautiful, inspirational meaningful place. Others will say it is people who make a difference, especially those who are enjoyable company, interesting in conversation, inspirational in their interests.

CREATING A DIFFERENT LIFE STORY

A multifaceted conversation with ourselves and with others in our world becomes a continuing reality, as we grow older. There is a continual internal and interpersonal conversation about our identity. 'What am I going to do? Am I like them? Do I have to accept that I am an older person?' is the type of conversation we have when we look into the mirror.

Apart from a chronological identity, we create a story about ourselves, an identity in which self-worth, self-fulfilment and self-realisation are important components. The dialogue is not only between people but also within the self as one expression of identity will dominate another, perhaps only for a time, or in a permanent sense of identity this will shape the person's existence in the context of others who also play a part in shaping that person's identity.

There are strong pressures from without, and desires from within, to be young. This is particularly common as people age. While we once held positions of high status, we now have to accept, and adapt to, the changes in how we are perceived by others. The reality is that there will be times when each one of us tries to be someone they can never be again. In being over protective of what and who we once were, we may forfeit the person we have now become.

Uncertainty follows many people across their lifetime. What identity will give me the most stable satisfaction? From all the dialogical experiences of ageing, which identity will be most acceptable at different points across the life span? Close consideration will also be necessary to protect identity in times of quietness and after times of disruption and decline. It is common to find that little planning or research has gone towards effective protections of identity.

AVOIDING THE BLUES

Despite our growing interest in the psychology of human happiness, in the later stages of our life, the shadows of human pessimism can become persuasively and intermittently dominant. The tendency to focus on the psychological pathologies that may be involved can mean that the study of the healthy aged person can be given less attention. It is important to recognise, identify, and pay close attention to the characteristics of the healthy older person. It is in this way that we can create a greater awareness of the possibilities for ourselves and encourage a greater engagement in contexts which are affirming and in which we can find fulfilment.

Many maintain a strong sense of who they once were, particularly through their lifetime of service in their professions, or through the warmth and stimulation of an intimate relationship. Some shun that possibility, finding enjoyment instead through the bond established with companion animals, such as dogs. Others avoid despairing by declaring that the past is past, by making a commitment to keeping healthy and fit, reflecting on the gift of life, and pursuing a desire to live life well. By reorganising and developing, self-strengths, self-enjoyments and self-satisfactions, despair can be avoided.

COPING WITH DESPAIR

When despair sets in it can be insidiously demoralising, particularly as we grow older. Recognising despair, noting its onset, manifestations and possible consequences, may go some of the way to preventing the emotions and behaviours of despair, intercepting them and minimising the damage they can do. They are: depression, alcohol dependency, addictions, chronic resentments, anger or rage, boredom, social emptiness, relationship dysfunction, spiritual meaninglessness, and the subtleties of the death wish.

These conditions may occur as specific and separate concerns, or they may be manifested in various co-morbidities. Some, like depression, alcohol dependence and rage may occur together, while a condition like spiritual meaninglessness may be dismissed as an irrelevance, as its subtle containment and its stereotyping of resilience may go unrecognised. These conditions can be prevented. They all play a significant part in human happiness, human relationships, and human survival, and a diminishing interest in life expectancy.

Ways to Sustain Positive Self Esteem

1. Identify people and relationships that are supportive and affirming.
2. Identify and value emotions of laughter, enjoyment, and inspirational pursuits.
3. Participate in groups and organisations that expand a sense of belonging and a positive purpose, and achievement.
4. Recognise memories of life affirming experiences, and people who have or are strong models of affirmation.
5. A developed capacity to withstand experiences that threaten to undermine one's sense of value and purpose.
6. A capacity to contain anxieties and to manage them constructively.

DEALING WITH DEPRESSION

Many older people become depressed. Some would say that the circumstances and the troubles of old age would make some form of depression inevitable. We know that the depressions of old age can be prevented and effectively treated — with and without medication. Some depressions may become so deeply part of a person's coping that supervised medication is essential and can be effective in bringing a person back into the flow of life again. Other forms of depression can be relieved by the 'talking therapies' that refocus life directions and resources, that restore perspective on difficult problems, and that can reorganise a person's strengths and coping capacities. Some depressions can be effectively prevented by sustaining the resources of self-strengths, by reducing anxieties, and by engaging effective support.

From early childhood, there is a need for strong social belonging and cohesion, strong beliefs and affirmation of oneself, close bonds of non-judgemental acceptance and experiences of enjoyment, expectation and excitement in constructing a positive participation in the future. Where positive early childhood experiences are lacking, or have been lost, some planned assistance and support may be necessary to give that person a continuing experience of their place and importance, and of their expansiveness and resilience through their adult years and into old age.

Depression at any age can be overwhelming. Vigilance and compassion are necessary to ensure that prevention is both believable and carefully accessible. It is commonly an expression of 'closing down', 'closing in' and losing a free contact with others and a generous compassion for oneself. Depression can be an insidious and disguised condition. It may be influenced by experiences of failure, fears of failure, and the aggregation of anxieties related to current and earlier stresses over a long period of time. The loss of positive self-thoughts, the collapse of a rational perspective, the loss of belief in oneself, and the interpersonal environments, may rapidly lead to loss of commitment to the future and one's place within that future.

HEALING AND HOPE

While there is wide recognition of the dangers of depression, many fail to recognise how depression can be prevented and managed more effectively. Careful attention is recommended to identify symbols of healing and hope, to listen to music that lifts the human spirit, to be involved in activities that continue to transform moods, and give meaning to social interest and social engagements.

The seven big factors of personality give strong emphasis to the factors that promote hope. These include openness, commitment to self and others, expansiveness and positive energy, affability and acceptance, searching for new possibilities, and new inspirational resources and causes that give added meaning and purpose to life. Other factors that engender healing the depressive state include daily exercise, regular exposure to enjoyable events, joining with others in experiences that are expansive and deepening for the human spirit.

We all age in difference ways. Most commonly, there is the expectation and the anxiety of decline. While many find ways to soften and conceal the ubiquitous decline in our physical appearance, the major anxiety for most people is the decline in cognitive functioning. This includes the unreliability of memory, the uncertainties of direction and location, the loss of the mental capacity to process everyday information and requirements, and the loss of meaningful communication with people and their various environments.

Decline may affect many areas of living. Early detection of decline in specific areas may slow down and reduce the fear and anxiety that an overall decline is taking place. There is general recognition that the loss of physical fitness and changes in physical appearance associated with ageing can be prevented by observing regular physical exercise, balanced diets, reduction of stressful living and stressful circumstances.

Often, there is a decline in social engagement, and a loss of desire to socially interact. Sometimes this may be an indication of an incipient depression, an attitude of 'I can't be bothered', and 'hell is other people' as Jean Paul Sartre once commented. Maintaining social relationships, even within one's family can be stressful, especially when family members are not supportive, hostile, jealous or lacking in basic affability.

CONTAINING NEGATIVE EMOTIONS

A loss in social connectedness may also lead to a loss of enjoyment with others, and a general subjective wellbeing declines. People in older years may experience a decline in their sense of belonging and purpose, their life-meaning, and their identity and worth. This may be part of a decline in ethical and spiritual values of caring and compassion of human kindness and mutual enhancement and confirmation.

Decline may affect any and all of these areas, yet maintaining an inner sense of being in control of one's life may reduce the overall fear of decline. Identifying specific areas of decline, and taking action to reduce or control that decline in the specific area, may increase the likelihood of reducing the anxiety of decline overall. Where the more general decline is already occurring the progress and spread of that decline may be reduced when specific areas of decline can be identified and acted upon.

The management and containment of our emotions particularly, the emotions and moods of gloom and depression, of frustration and anger, of guilt and self-attack, become paramount. One way of addressing decline is in a therapeutic or supportive context. It is here that an ongoing assessment and discussion around feelings, functioning, focus, fantasy of the future, can take place. It is helpful to learn how to filter out negativities and filter in some effective positives; to fence-off areas of known destructiveness and demoralisation, and explore ways to sustain the positive flow of life.

AGEING WITH DIGNITY

Families will encounter the conflict between an obligation to care for their ageing parents and the reality that ageing parents have become inconveniently demanding and difficult. Although there are strong tendencies to avoid and deny the realities, families find they no longer like the behaviour of their parents or the physical and mental state that have become a daily burden. Mobility problems, hearing loss, general hygiene, chronic illness and constant complaining about everything and anything make the obligations sources of resentment. Many are able to reduce their own feelings of resentment by reassurances that this is the common lot of families attending to the needs and demands of ageing parents. Others realise that tolerance and caring must become part of an accepted obligation and reality.

Some families do not like what they hear and see. They realise they do not like their parents who have become unlikeable. They become unable to separate the person from the behaviour, the present from the past. It may be difficult to accept the reality that the person they once knew has undergone a slow or dramatic change. But recognition of these realities can become a major part of managing both their parents' situation and their conflicted feelings. Often, many carers and family members resent the reality.

While elderly parents rely on their family accepting their responsibilities, their likes and dislikes may be largely ignored. Elderly parents are ready to let their growing hostility about ageing be concealed behind the family obligation, which also protects them from the reality that they have become unlikeable. If older people are able to understand and accept the aspects of themselves that have become unlikeable, they may be able to intercept their behaviour and join in the important task of sustaining more tolerable environments.

In this chapter I explored the emotional challenges and pitfalls facing us as we age. What follows is a discussion of the importance of spirituality in our lives, the role it plays in overcoming loneliness, finding meaning, and maintaining contentment. The emphasis is on our 'three' brains working together in harmony. It involves engaging in emotional regulation, staying in the moment, letting go of regrets, getting over hurts, forgiving others, maintaining and losing friendships, and moving on.

Chapter 3

Spirituality and Contentment

People often sit with me and tell me the joys of their older years. They also tell me how they fear old age and its realities. Some have been angry for years and cannot find release for their resentments. Some are jammed up with things long past, and others scratch over their ant beds of discontent and disillusionment. Finding contentment is a challenge for every one of us.

THE HUMAN BRAIN IN THREE PARTS

Our brain can be described in three parts: the emotional brain; the rational brain; the spiritual brain. We become whole human beings to the extent that these three brains work together in harmony. Our feelings and rational reasoning changes everything. We know how our emotions can run all over the place. We know how our emotions, when they are under control, can bring great experiences in our relationships, in our music, in our art, and in our achievements.

We know that our rational brain is so important to us, to recognise the right path, to get beyond our disillusionment and destructiveness, and to bring inspiration to our lives and relationships. What of the spiritual brain? It comes to us and it leaves us. It comes to us and calms us. It comes to us and enhances our creativity. It comes to us and shows us that kindness is better. It comes to us and points to Faith, Hope, and Love. Without these, life is less.

THE EMOTIONAL AND RATIONAL BRAIN

We all carry around a bag of emotions that I call our emotional brain. The potential of good expansive beautiful emotions is in there. This bag can carry negative emotions, of inferior feelings, of angry feelings. All are often concealed or covered over by our dislike of other people, or the fear each day might uncover. The emotional brain can be the greatest gift where positive feelings, beautiful experiences, and good memories abound. Often the emotional brain can be irrational, and uncontrollable and self-damaging in its self-destructiveness and hurtfulness of others. The task is to harness these tangled and tangling emotions.

After years, after a lifetime of being tormented by our emotional brain, the rational brain can intervene. The rational brain can tell us that there is a better way, another way, a healthier way, a more successful enjoyable way. The emotional brain and the rational brain can entangle each other. We need the third brain to bring some quietness to our mind, to our life, to our relationships with people, to our relationships with the world.

THE SPIRITUAL BRAIN

The third brain is the spiritual brain, which comes to remind the emotional and rational brain of the great gifts of memory, the great moments of life, and the profound difference it makes when we embrace a positive meaning for our life. Memory, meaning, moments, all working in harmony with the emotional brain, the rational brain, the spiritual brain, three brains working together. It is like waking from a deep sleep, feeling something is not right. And then you realise that your blanket has slipped off. You pull that blanket back on and you feel the difference — the blanket of warmth and quietness, the blanket of contentment and calm, the essential blanket.

Many people cannot be bothered thinking about the spiritual, yet we all see a good spirit and we like that. We all search for a good spirit in our workplace. We all would like to strengthen a good spirit in our relationships. We all would like to celebrate a good spirit in the world. It is always so much better than the angry spirit which can jump on top of us and make a distressing mess for days. It is so much better than the inferiority spirit that can make us feel less than we are.

One thing above all is vital. We need to focus on something beyond ourselves, something of ultimate importance. The good spirit is something that makes us feel grateful and good, feel alive, feel part of the celebration of life. It brings its friends:

- the friend of forgiveness.
- the friend of cooperation.
- the friend of kindness.

The good spirit is a gift. The good spirit is something we can search out and strengthen. It is the idea of a good spirit in your life, in your midst.

Search for it. When you see it, strengthen it, study it, celebrate it. It changes everything. When you become part of the good spirit, when the good spirit becomes part of you, everything changes.

THERAPEUTIC SPIRITUALITY

The 23rd Psalm is probably one of the most recognised pieces of Scripture. In pondering the existential anxieties, the psalmist turns to the image of a shepherd caring for his sheep, calm waters, and a cup overflowing. These images can be translated into images that can be meaningful, by recognising the existential anxieties of the psalmist are also ours.

Generous Giver of all things: in your presence my inner spirit is fully satisfied. I know I share in the abundance of life. I can lie down without fear. I can sit beside the stillness of the river. I find my soul strengthened. I know there are right paths. My God will guide me to them.

I know I must face the shadows of life and meet my death. I will do so with courage. I know there is an unseen presence with me that gives me comfort.

Generous Giver, along with all the uncertainties and threats of life, you provide me with good gifts. When I have enough, you pour into my life something more. Indeed: my cup overflows.

May I find and give goodness and kindness every day of my life. Let my life be a constant expression of my desire to reflect your good presence wherever I am, wherever I go. Wherever. Forever.

For me, the psalm spells out the ingredients of what I call 'Therapeutic Spirituality'. It points to a strengthening of the human spirit, a softening, steadying of the spirit. It speaks of the presence of the spirit, protection of the spirit, the plan of the spirit — spiritual people, spiritual places, spiritual moments, spiritual meaning. The state of the human spirit is vital, its strength, its support, sensitivity, its search for something that will make a difference. A good spirit — see it; search for it; study it; strengthen it; celebrate it.

EMOTIONAL LONELINESS

Loneliness is a basic part of all human existence. From earliest childhood there is considerable encouragement for children to form and sustain emotional bonds first with parents and family members, with pets and peers. Some people describe how they have always felt lonely, distant, unconnected, whether in their relationships with others, in the world of their pets, or in all that the world offers. As we grow older, and into old age, we may find ourselves confronted with the ache of loneliness. Others find that life takes a different course, they are never troubled by loneliness or what people think about them.

In its various manifestations, loneliness is the awareness of an existential alienation from others, from the core harmony of existence, from one's self-potential and the capacity and courage to actualise that potential. Being in a relationship, whether it is with intimates or work colleagues may not decrease our loneliness. The relationship may be one of business and purpose, with little attention to the vital needs of empathy and kindness, of soothing and support, of enjoyment and shared inspiration.

Enjoyable connections and our belongings to various aspects of life may lead to a more meaningful existence. But their absence, or unpredictability, may lead to an unmistakable emotional ache. I often hear it said that being with others is a lonelier experience than being alone.

There are many calls to surround older people with friendly supportive relationships. The practical reality is that family may claim that regularly visiting the aged is not experienced as enjoyable for the visitor or the visited. Family members will find there is little to talk about, and the grumbling of the elderly becomes a source of dissatisfaction. Being part of an institution may give the impression that there is ample room for social connection. In fact, having many people around does not guarantee a lessening of the ache of loneliness or alleviate its painful aspects.

LETTING GO OF REGRETS

We all have regrets. Mistakes were made, a relationship broke down or never eventuated, a beautiful moment was spoilt. We ponder what could have been. What we wished for never happened. A regret may have its natural narrative — something happened; it had painful consequences; we wish it had not happened; we regret the aftermath. Alternatively, the happening in itself does not provoke regret — it happened. We accept that it happened, or agree what regrets will be accepted. A new way forward is developed.

A regret carries a heightened awareness of what occurred. It involves an appraisal of the damage, the feelings associated with it, and the people involved. It requires an evaluation of the extent of the damage, the possibilities of reparation, the people, personalities and the relationships involved. And it involves a reappraisal of our past and future relationships. Many older people recognise these experiences and carry many regrets for what occurred, and for the management of what occurred.

This is not surprising given that we often spend a lot of our time simply remembering as we age. Regrets may arise not only from the thoughts of events that occurred, but from what did not occur, 'If only I had remembered... Life would have been very different if...' Many speculations are drawn together to help explain why certain things happened and other things did not happen. Was it 'chance', the alignment of the stars, an unseen presence guiding us, or were we unconsciously drawn to this person and repelled by that one. Regrets are sealed into memories. Jonathan said he regrets the mistakes but Jennifer said, 'Does he really regret what he did? Can we ever trust him again? Who forgets?'

Regrets rarely evaporate quickly. The original offence calls out for ownership. Its powerful destructiveness recognised, given words, and thereby finds a new positioning in our memory and in our psyche, and its years of pain, softened. The event of the past resists that softening, and we must consider whether we can build and embrace softening in ourselves. Much as we would like to erase every shadow of a painful past, that is not possible. Many apologies may be called upon — when the tree has been burnt, it cannot be unburnt; when an arm has been severed, it cannot usually be un-severed; when words have been spoken, they cannot be unspoken; after a life has been lost, it cannot be unlost.

FORGIVING OTHERS

'I hate myself for what I did back then.' A man, aged 62, reflected on the way he behaved towards his two older sisters at a time when they were attempting to resolve their disagreements regarding their father's estate. For 26 years he had been holding onto his regrets. If only a sincerely worded apology — written and spoken — could erase the memory, lift his regret, or better still, cancel the events altogether so that the original innocence that once existed could be reinstated.

His sisters had been deeply wounded by his words and his behaviour. They said they would forgive him, but they could never forget how he had destroyed that precious unity of their family. In himself, he realised that he had hurt them and had fallen far short of the values he thought he held. Not only did he feel hated by his sisters, but also he hated himself. They would never see each other again. His inner remorse could be somewhat placated by an inner resolve to 'get on with life', and refuse to allow himself to think of the part that he had played in destroying his family relationships.

Sometimes, a sense of self-righteousness seemed to give him permission to hate his sisters, and his deceased father. After 26 years of self-hate, he decided to tell someone — his therapist — about it. 'I have never told anyone about how I really feel,' he said. His eyes welled-up with tears, and as he coughed, he apologised. Still unable to face his past, he seemed more concerned about this show of 'weakness' in the present.

The man has the task to reshape his life — aware that some parts of the past can never be changed. The sisters have the task of reshaping their lives aware of the damage done by their brother. Some people, conscious of what they have done in the past, or what the past has done to them, begin to live in a small safe 'place'. Others, as if to prove their possibilities, construct big lives and large places. Some are driven by the energy of the strong emotions, others live with their emotional blinds drawn all day.

In the vast plethora of joys and sorrows that

can happen to any one person, we come to realise that it is not possible to explain why we turned left on 'that day' 20 years ago. We read countless biographies, watch films of how life happened to this one or to that community. We read poetry, and we ponder the meaning of not taking 'The Road Less Travelled'. There are many who missed even that road. Perhaps they must settle for the sheer truculence of life, be embittered by it, or find a way to face and to resolve what needs to be faced, with courage and resilience.

People need help, discernment, and support, as they explore the courage and resilience acceptable to them. If they abandon that search, regret may be replaced by a deepening sense of loss, the emptiness of life and deepening despair. Rather than remain in that emptiness, the person may construct and reshape different activities in which meaning and fulfilment may be found. It means to take the solemnity of the many regrets that cannot be reversed, and claim some self-affirmation, in spite of what happened, or did not happen. The negative posture of regret can be transcended by the awareness and construction of a positive emotion.

MEMORIES

We tend to take our mind for granted, that is until we can't remember. Until it does not function as it once did. The mind leaves us worrying over trivial things. The mind distorts some good experiences into misery. Our own mind can rush us into confusion and panic, and it can take us into the most beautiful experiences. Some people serve the world in life-saving ways by training their minds to perform the most intricate tasks.

The mind can be developed to be engaged in very specialised activities or to do routine, rote tasks every day; or it can deteriorate and become unpredictable and uncontrollable. Many discover that this highly valuable 'control station' can lose many of its functions that provide people with their identity, direction, belonging, and their mental functioning, and their mental health. It is such a vital part of our life, but we know so little about it, and we are largely unaware of how to preserve our mind in good health.

As we age, our memory begins to dominate our anxieties. 'I think I'm losing my memory.' 'I can't remember what happened two days ago, but I'm often going over memories of things that happened 60 years ago.' 'There are things — try as I do — I can't remember. And there are other things I wish I could forget'. 'Some things were so unpleasant, I don't want to remember. Other events were so enjoyable I wish I could remember them in all their detail. But what's the point?'

Perhaps I have to control my memories and say, 'What's past is past! I must let the past be past'. This suggests that the person has control over their memories, but in reality, they may be unable to sleep because memories of the past persist in the tyranny of their mind. Memory can be an exhilarating mystery when two very old people, having not seen each other for decades, meet and recall enjoyable events of their shared childhood. On the other hand, people on trial in the courts, asked to recall distressing events of a year earlier, claim that they have no memory of the event.

It is noteworthy that the psychological talking professions, which focus so constantly on relieving distressing memories, have often given unreliable and confusing information on memories. They have largely accepted that memory activity happens without the conscious control of the person. A mother has a vivid memory of her six-year-old daughter being hit and killed by a speeding vehicle.

She repeatedly recalls many details of the tragedy; in times of quiet relaxation, a sudden flashback occurs; she reads newspaper accounts of similar tragedies; a brief scene occurring on the television news can re-invoke the memory and the distress that surrounds it.

NEGATIVE MEMORIES

Some memories are so dominant that they resist any attempt to forget them. A conscious decision to delete the memory will be dismissed as impossible. In various explorations of brain and memory function, it is well known that some memories are deleted: the person cannot remember. A protest may be made — 'But you were "there". Of course you must remember'. Was the deletion of the memory due to inattention failure? Was it due to the pain being so intense that the memory was repressed?

We know that some form of deletion can occur. In some instances this is done consciously when the person declares that they have the memory of a certain event or events. In other instances, the claim may be made that it occurred long ago. It is said that this event was confused with other events occurring at the time. In everyone's experience, many of life's memories are deleted or placed in a kind of 'recess'. That the memory itself is temporarily or permanently outside any conscious recall. Under some circumstances the memories may be returned to consciousness, but in the passing of time and everyday events, they are forgotten.

Memory distress commonly arises from the tyranny of bad memories. To prevent memories from dominating or tyrannising thought and behaviour they can be controlled. Commonly, a person might say, 'I just can't get to sleep', or 'I get to sleep and an hour later, I am awake, going over the memories of how I was treated, the injustices, the nasty behaviour'. Restraining is similar to blocking and suppressing. A primary objective is to recognise that the memory is controllable, and by using conscious strategies or forms of imagery, relaxation and mind quietening, the tyranny of the memory can be settled.

REPOSITIONING MEMORIES

Sometimes people will need some help to be released from their ruminations about the past, to reposition their memories so that some can slip into oblivion, and others can continue to be valued enrichments of their identity, belonging, and gratitude. Some memories can hold people in a chronic negative return to the past. They may not speak about their past, but it may continue to affect their health, enjoyment of life and relationships. It is not uncommon that one negative memory will — in effect — search out other negative memories and so a life of negative retrospectivity can become part of a larger picture of injustice, resentment and unrelieved personal and social pain.

How does a parent cope with the murder of their children 30 years ago? With the passing of time, the pain spreads to so many areas of unlived moments, of deprivation, of unforgivable injustice, of unrelieved pain. While for some, the retrospective life is a wasted life, for others such a life is one of dreadful sympathy for suffering that is embedded forever in memory, loneliness, and unrelieved sorrow.

Memories are organised and stored within and around the functioning self. Memory gives meaning to the identity of the self, and the self sustains the organisation of memory. Without a coherent sense of self, memories become chaotic. This is relevant to all ages. It is particularly so for people experiencing the anxiety of their older years. The awareness and symptoms of memory loss and deterioration are a source of considerable anxiety. Recognising the function of memory provides some basis for exercising some effective and preventative control over memory functioning, rather than succumbing to a passive acceptance of 'Whatever happens, happens'.

It is important to practise filtering out your toxic memories and filtering in good memories. Your good memories enhance your identify — who you are — remind you of good places and good people. Good memories bring a sense of enjoyment and enlargement to existence. They are able to bring you a sense of who you 'were' and who you 'are'. Frequently you will hear people say, 'That does not make sense'. Life has lost its meaning.

The task is to re-find meaning in your life. Without that sense of meaning and purpose you are vulnerable to depression, disgruntlement, and disillusionment. For some, meaning and purpose come easily — perhaps their family relationships spontaneously explore events that give life its positive meaning. For others, it is difficult to find a satisfactory meaning in anything. Most people come to realise that meaning does not 'just happen'. They have to give meaning to a difficult experience. They might have to impose meaning on a meaningless event.

POSITIVE MEMORIES

An event occurs. The event in the past moment becomes, or is given, a memory. That memory may have the power to give that past event life into the future. We can select our memories. We recall a stressful or hurtful event. It carries a distressing memory. Will we hold onto the memory and its distress? Is it possible to select another event, with a 'good' memory? Can we hold onto that memory and its positive emotion? As we verbalise this process, we recognise pathways that may be developed and expanded in the future.

Some memories are harsh and painful, and a person remembers the valued and beautiful personality of one who has died. A transformation of the painful memory is possible as the person receives condolences and assurances of support and the pain is softened and soothed. Memories are a basic part of human identity, of who we are as functioning selves. It is possible to select good memories; to imagine and construct good memories, which will carry positive feelings, positive rewards, and make living into the future more enjoyable.

To many people, asking the question, 'Do you want to have good memories or bad memories?' may evoke some anxiety. But asking the question brings an essential focus to thought and behaviour. 'Do you recognise that bad memories come from your experience of "bad" events and from the negative emotions and meanings that adhere to those experiences of bad events?'

INSPIRATIONAL MEMORIES

It is possible to construct good events that will yield good memories? Remembering and forgetting, along with fantasy and inspiration, are aspects of mind and behaviour that continue to be misunderstood and unpredictable. Some people would like to forget what is too vividly remembered, and some are sensitive to their awareness that they have forgotten what they had wanted to remember. Although memory is vital to everyone's everyday living, it is notable how profoundly ignorant everyone is about how the ageing brain functions and of memory management.

Individual differences in many areas of interpersonal behaviour increase the complexity of understanding how memory is affected as people age. It is common to hear talk of the deterioration and unreliability of short term memory and how long term memory remains intact. Little is known about the way memory is sustained by the activation of positive emotions, how positive memories can be obliterated by a traumatic experience, how we are fastidious about keeping the appointment with our dentist, but forget the lunch engagement with an acquaintance.

Why is there resistance to recognising inspiration as a significant influence, and the memory of these influences as a known factor in human behaviour? Wide recognition and study have been given to the traumatic life-changing aspects of memory. At the same time, little sustained attention or research has been given to the inspirational aspects of memory. Yet, people, places, ideas, poetry and music have been sources of inspiration and behaviour for centuries. Our achievements, character formation, group behaviour and political movements are initiated and sustained by an inspirational person or event. The memory of that person or event remains a significant influence on how we live our life, the choices we make, our sense of well-being, and our behaviour.

MAKING A CHOICE TO BE HAPPY

Everyone wants to be happy. If we are happy, we

are usually better company and more likely to function better. Happy individuals bring a positive focus into their lives and they are likely to cope better with the changes involved with growing old. Some will say they are happier today than they were yesterday. They are happier in this time of their life than they were when they were young. They might name the things that make them unhappy or that threaten their happiness, but they may not be able to be confident in naming the predictors of their happiness.

A person may continue to be unhappy, believing they have no alternative. Others recognise that the circumstances and events of life would cause them to be unhappy, but they choose to be happy. To remain in an unhappy state can have multiple ongoing consequences. Choosing to be happy, in spite of what has occurred, has the potential to change the perception and management of the circumstance, one's sense of control, and one's wellbeing.

We need to intercept our unhappiness, and purposefully explore ways to re-instate some happiness. It is possible for a person to make up their mind to be happy. It is possible to be happy when many negative factors of old age tend to dominate. While decisions around happiness may be difficult to make, making a conscious choice to be happy means, among other things, that we like ourselves more and we like others in our world more too. Recognising some of the predictors of happiness may mean that some action can be taken to strengthen the experiences of happiness in older years.

Predictors of Happiness

1. Our behaviour towards ourselves, and other people's behaviour towards us, can be a source of happiness.
2. Our environments and circumstances can be factors that predict happiness — when we are in those environments and part of specific circumstances, we are able to recognise their contribution to happiness in ourselves, and also in others.
3. Our way of interpreting events and our emotional response to events will play a major part in our happiness and unhappiness.
4. Past experiences and the emotional investments we give to those past experiences will be factors of our happiness.
5. Learning how to filter out negative or troublesome memories and filtering in good memories, to identify quiet places to remember good events — the capacity to be released from

resentment, regrets and remorse.

6. Various stimuli can be recognised as part of transformative experiences — music, art, poetry, thoughtful and caring words, occasions of celebration, travel, visiting new places, contributing to good causes.

CREATING JOY

Joy is something that is often present when we are younger. But in our older years, joy takes many different forms. It can be evasive. It can be concealed. It will be lost under the dominance of many negative emotions, distressing mistakes, and miserable relationships. In older age, a person needs to keep joy alive. What will sustain a sense of joy in old age? When joy is lost, how will it be recovered? Such questions are likely to assume that joy is a basic goal of ageing. But is this so?

When old age is examined for its joy, we see two faces of joy. On the one hand studies indicate that old and very old people record a sustained sense of happiness and wellbeing. On the other hand, some individuals will describe numerous instances of feeling diminished or lost. As the loss of joy affects the many aspects of living, it is difficult to provide a one-solution-fits-all. Without a specific approach to the recovery of joy, the tendency is to dismiss joy as an achievable scientific objective, or to speak of it in such general terms that there may be little specific application.

There is the trend to use such terms as 'happiness' and 'subjective well-being' and thus avoid the use of the word 'joy' altogether. We need to decide if subjective wellbeing is synonymous with joy, or whether joy is something more. Colloquially, people speak of 'losing the joy of living'. Is that saying that they are depressed, or is it a statement about the loss of positive emotions?

Many aspects of a person's everyday life are to be enjoyed: work, peer relationships, marriage and family, sporting activities and hobbies. Many of these activities become necessities so that other aspects of our lives can be enjoyed. One person may say they do not get joy from their work, but it is a necessity that provides money to pay the rent for a house they enjoy, or for taking the children on a summer holiday, which they also enjoy. Another person will sacrifice joy in one area in order to experience joy in another area. Creating joy involves being open to the following:

How to Be Joyful

1. Open the pathways for joy to flow.
2. Seal off negative emotions.

3. Strengthen the softened places.
4. Strengthen the healing directions:
    - behave joyfully.
    - speak joyful words.
    - welcome joyful feelings.
    - read joyful stories.
    - listen to joyful music, joyful songs.
    - choose joyful relationships.
    - recognise the joyful moments.
    - walk in joyful (joy-giving) places.
    - write joyful letters (words).
    - set up joyful memorial turning points.
5. Reinvest in images of the recovered resilient self.
6. Explore the dynamics of faith and memory.
7. Invest in images of emotional enrichment.

RECOVERING JOY

Recovering a sense of joy involves both external and internal rearrangements and reconstruction. The externals may include changing work commitments, re-evaluation and reconstruction of relationships, purchasing a desired object, holidaying in an overseas country, becoming successful in learning a musical instrument. Internal concerns that affect the sense of joy might include adaptation to loss and change across the life span, being open to new experiences, being an active participant in good causes, reducing neurotic tendencies and neurotic behaviours.

Recovering joy requires 'fencing-off' negative and painful experiences, resolving to avoid some situations and people, and making choices that maximise the possibilities of joy even in circumstances of difficulty and sorrow. Emotional regulation involves dealing with the following:

Emotional Regulation

1. Disappointments, failures and past mistakes.
2. Conflict and dissatisfaction in past and current relationships.
3. Difficulties adapting to ageing, to change and losses associated with ageing.
4. Uncontained words and emotions.
5. Loss of identity, purpose and passion in life.
6. Unsettled memories of past events.
7. Inability to sustain satisfying mutually enriching relationships.
8. Inability to sustain effective ways to live the years of retirement.
9. Resistance to relinquishing resentments.

GAINING INSIGHT

Feeling directionless is common as we age and yet it is commonly denied. But there is gratitude when something or someone turns up to engage us for a time. There is a growing awareness that such activities will be temporary or transitory, and in their passing they leave us to wonder what may emerge tomorrow. Perhaps an unconscious anxiety creates an emptiness where tomorrow is not a consideration. For many, emptiness can be filled for a time with what happened, and what we did, and what we achieved yesterday.

The retrospective life can be a comfort for a time, but it does not enjoy a long shelf life, especially as friends begin to show a declining interest in hearing the same stories again and again. Often people seem to lose their capacity to register how often they have repeated themselves and to whom. Friends and interested audiences show a generous benevolence as they patiently listen, and at times pretend that they have not heard the story before.

The story may be of a holiday 30 years ago, of a marriage that they might have had, the achievements of their parents, or events that happened many years previously. But the story may be of a hurt they suffered from one who is long since deceased, or of a quarrel that they had in an organisation years ago. They can be recalling or retelling of experiences of childhood, the love of a parent, or the harsh treatment of an adoptive family.

MANAGING ANXIETIES

Affability at any age will be preferred to unpredictable aggression. In old age, affability may become a benign admission that quietness, even blandness, is preferred to expressions of impatience and irritability. There is a view that old people should be actively and enjoyably engaged in forward-looking activity, but another view is that an affable, directionless, retrospective life, has protections against anxiety. If happiness is part of that life, is that sufficient? A major persisting task of old age is adaptation — adapting to change and loss, adapting to different sources of happiness.

Most older people find ways to contain their anxieties and cope with them. But many worry continuously about how they will cope with 'what is ahead of them', and others worry about what will happen to their adult children after they die. There are losses of family and friends. There is sadness and sorrow, financial worries and the unmistakable and mounting signs of deterioration and decline emerge.

Some have been swept into the anxieties of wartime upheaval and natural disasters. Others are dealing with the immediacy of illness and injury, loss of confidence, and the strength to sustain adequate interpersonal affirmations and the vital softeners against the harsh realities of their existence. By naming common anxieties, we take some first steps to contain and control these anxieties.

Common Anxieties

1. The anxieties of inadequacy, of self evaluation and self-devaluation, self-worth and self-enjoyments; the anxieties of searching for a sense of significance.
2. The anxieties of social approval, social affirmation, social support, social engagement and social enjoyment.
3. The search for satisfaction with oneself, satisfaction about past pursuits and achievements, satisfaction in relationships, and satisfaction in one's direction in life.
4. The anxiety of insecurity and the search for a sense of security, adapting to the realities of life, as they are, and as they are perceived.
5. The anxieties of successful adaptation to

the contexts of self, family, work, play, and retirement.

6. The anxiety of competence and skills for the requirements of life, living with others, living in the world.
7. The anxieties about loss of relationships, and loss of self-functioning.
8. The anxiety of finding the softeners and soothers for the difficult pains of existence.
9. The anxiety of finding and sustaining a loving and enriching relationship and/or a satisfying investment in an enriching pursuit.

MAINTAINING GOOD RELATIONSHIPS

The importance of living and loving have long been recognised as the pillars on which emotional security are built. Our adult relationships have various levels of intensity and commitment. But they do have one thing in common: feelings of being loved and being special. Some relationships are casual, superficially touching, or bonded by shared interests. Others demand totalitarianism and may ultimately be governed more by fear than by enjoyment. Our relationships may be strong as they affirm the individuality of each person. Or they may exist tenuously on the basis of verbal assurance, rather than a sharing of interests and concerns.

A friendship may arise from a common belonging to a political party, a church, a sporting club, but various calculations apply. In belonging to one group, how much will we disclose of our belonging to another group, will we involve families, or is it wiser to observe certain boundaries of engagement; will we give gifts and how much will we spend, and how often will we meet? Is friendship dependent on frequency of contact or the commonality of interest? In friendship, whom can we count on, and count on for what?

We might feel comfortable in counting on a friend to collect our mail when we are on holidays, but not too often. We can count on them to drive us to golf, but not if they have been drinking alcohol. When can we count on our friends, for what, how often? In times of serious illness, the support of reliable friends can be a valuable aid to our recovery, but if our friends do not volunteer to help, what can we do? If we asked them for help, they might well say they do not have the energy to do so, that they have to figure out what they can do in their own lives.

As we age, many friendships are lost,

new friendships may be formed. The nature of friendship may change and be sustained by an occasional e-mail, or the surprise meeting at a funeral. Some friendships may be inactive or non-existent for years, but in times of need, they may become a 'convoy' of friends, providing valued support and protection. They may be hard to find and be subject to misunderstanding and unreliability, not least because neither party to the friendship has recognised the purposes that they thought friendship served. Women may find friendship with other women that provide enjoyment and support. Friendships between men and women are likely to carry a level of anxiety as to the function of such friendships and how they might be interpreted by the social world.

MALE FRIENDSHIPS

Despite having interests in various areas of life, many men say they have very few friends, or none at all. Some say they 'can't be bothered'; others are 'too busy'. Some will say they have to be with their wife, and others that their 'knees are playing up', and others have become accustomed to being uninvolved, never were involved and feel awkward trying to become involved. Many settle for a level of superficial involvement, accepting that this is the way things are — 'this is as good as it gets'.

Is it important for men to have men friends? What function do such friendships serve? How do men sustain their friendships, or how do they live with limited or no friendships? Men may marry and have children. For some years, the anxiety of friendship is settled. But in older years, do older men settle for being old and grumpy, old and boring, or old and co-dependent on individual family members? Friendships in older years have several vital functions:

THE IMPORTANCE OF FRIENDSHIPS

1. They help to define our identity — who we are and who we are not; who is important to us, and how we value others.
2. Friendships are expressions of caring about others, and for others, and about who and what they care.
3. Friendship in older years reminds us of our common inadequacies and anxieties, and of our common supports and strengths.
4. Friendships provide protection against the anxieties of loneliness and emptiness, of

meaninglessness, and mortality.

5. Friendships challenge our narcissistic preoccupations, and provoke acceptance and tolerance of others in older years.
6. Friendships encourage openness to social interests, social engagement and social enjoyment.
7. Friendships provide ongoing awareness of exploring life's meanings and satisfactions in a context where genuine relationships are sought.
8. Friendships consist of outgoing circles of closeness marked by expanding and contracting experiences of giving and taking.
9. Friendships that are valued and continuously nurtured contribute to life's quality, enjoyment, and generosity.

INTIMATE FRIENDSHIPS

In many subtle ways that defy adequate definition or description, friendships broaden and deepen the human being in ways beyond the cognitive and emotional experience. They become valued aspects of the spiritual core of the human experience. For some, they can become a narcissistic engulfment, a demand of an impoverished superego. But they can be part of the enlargement of mature relationships that are valued for the qualities they possess and that they bring to the relationship. They show respect for the individuality and differences in the other person or group, thereby not only accepting the other, but enhancing the self.

Some friendships need constant attention, while others can pick up where they left off years before. And there are those that drift away and are not renewed, or are once again remembered, as at a reunion. There are also those that rely heavily on empathy, while others may exist only by virtue of a common interest for a particular period of time. Friendships can outlive themselves, but memories may persist, augmented, in some cases, by a spiritual bond. The relationships we formed at school may in later years become a memory that can be recalled and discussed and, once again be stored away or dismissed.

In all their many complexities, our friendships may become divorced from the reality of the other person and become a distortion of the other, or a fantasy of what one once had, or would like to have. Indeed, they often become not about the other person as they actually are. Instead, they become part of the fiction of our desire, a fantasy that may be forever removed from the reality. A relationship always involves such a distortion, as we search for the person we would like, or imagine, the other person to be.

DEALING WITH CONFLICT IN FRIENDSHIPS

Friendship involves searching for and finding aspects of ourselves in the other person. Since no one can be free of interpersonal distortions, it is often a real struggle to sustain relationships when there is the inevitable contamination of distortion. It is common that in close friendships, as soon as we find them we close down the search, or we draw the boundaries of our relationship. Severe conflict can arise as one searches for the fantasy as distinct from the reality that is continually emerging. Wrongly, many people want to strip their relationships with others of all fantasy and illusion, so that they see the other 'as they really are'.

Harmony and disharmony are well-known factors of friendship. Most close relationships have times of discontent. There are a number of ways to reduce that discontent, and reverse its depressing difficulties. You might give the relationship a status check: do you want to sustain the relationship? What level of enthusiasm do you bring to it: Is it a relationship being loaded with disappointment and discontent? Make a clear decision about whether it is a relationship you want, or a relationship of quarrels and conflict.

EMOTIONAL LOADINGS

Another need is to balance the satisfactions against the dissatisfactions. If the dissatisfactions are greater than the satisfactions, that imbalance needs early attention. Each of the problems gathers an emotional loading — usually a loading of frustration and anger. We need to identify the problems and resist their tendency to run together. We need to separate the problem(s) from their emotional loading. Trying to deal with a 'problem' when it is loaded with anger or grief will probably mean that the problem and the emotion hinder the process of solving the problem.

It is important to regulate emotions by learning how to contain anger, anxiety and anguish. An overload of negative feelings will mean our functioning will be ineffective. We are likely to lose focus on what is of real importance. We stop filtering out negative thoughts, memories and emotions, and filter in the positives when what is required is to rediscover a good fantasy about the future, what you really want and what you need to do to keep that fantasy alive.

We all know that the tendency to revisit old 'hurts' can be very strong. We are likely to go back over things again and again. There is a need to resist the tendency — sometimes the obsession — to 'dig up old graves'. To overcome this we need to revisit our self worth, our self-strengths, and reposition our self-confidence. Positive people and influences make an enormous difference. They assist by confirming positive emotions and expressions of our personality.

DEALING WITH CHANGE IN FRIENDSHIPS

We need to recognise that friendships are constantly changing. A friend marries his friend's sister. Two friends go into a business partnership together, or purchase a house next door to each other. Friends 'fall-out' with each other when the daughter of one scooped all the school prizes; when one friend gives her newborn child the name that her friend was going to call her child; when the sons of two friends have become aggressively competitive. As a result, some people develop the symptoms of demoralisation and depression. They become angry and resentful that life and people have not been what they had hoped.

One difficulty or difference can end a friendship. A particular sensitivity will mean that the continuation of the friendship will depend on avoiding those areas of difference or downgrading the importance that might have been given to a particular concern. Much will depend on the capacity and understanding of adaptability and resilience if a damaged friendship is to survive and be enjoyed by both parties, free from the regressive influences of other audiences.

A commitment to some values or emotional needs may mean that a friendship will survive despite the injuries and inadequacies. Some might say, 'We are no longer friends in the way we were previously, but it is in everyone's interests for the partnership to continue.' Friends living next door or in the same neighbourhood, or belonging to the same church may continue their friendship with certain safeguards and conditions. They are unable to demand that a friend should leave the neighbourhood, but they can exercise some controls over how a different relationship will operate.

The parties were 'good friends', but that friendship may change into a necessary working relationship, without expectations or stimulations that were once seen as basic to friendship. In many instances, the unspoken task is to keep the friendship functioning, maximising contentment, and minimising discontent. When a relationship has been damaged, broken down, or burnt out, we are faced with a number of considerations. And we need the ability to embrace the following strengths:

Relationship Strengths

1. The strength to let go and refocus life directions.
2. The strength to accept that some things will not change.
3. The strength to bounce back and try again.
4. The strength to turn adversity to some advantage.
5. The strength to remain quiet when anxiety is at a high level.
6. The strength to accommodate other people without being overcome by their demands.
7. The strength to accept the reality of contradictions and stay focused on the best goals and outcomes.

NEW FRIENDSHIPS

Creating new friendships when we are older may be easy for some, as they discover and explore current and past interests and affiliations, achievements, and aspirations. For others, new friendships are difficult to create and difficult to sustain. Similar status, economic equality, and cultural sameness will be active factors for some, but for others, the strength of differences may draw people to each other.

Friendship at any phase of life relies on reciprocities of friendliness, reliability, and respect for assumed and stated rules and values. It is probably the case that people continue to establish friendships that will serve certain aspirational interests, but generally friendships develop out of common interests and casual contacts, waiting to see what emerges as reciprocal gestures are made.

Many have no clear ideas on how they will create friendships, how they will sustain friendships, how they will repair broken friendships, or how they will recover after the loss of friendships. Many male friendships are sustained even when they have long since lost their bonding energy. Some will say of their longstanding friends that they have become tiresome, boring, and burdensome as they begin to show the signs of deterioration. For others, there is a continued acknowledgement of the friendship, even though the frequency of contact may be reduced.

Despite the suspicion and fear that readily surface, males and females can and do have mutually rewarding friendships. While intimacy may be sustained throughout a marriage, many find a sense of intimacy in other areas of life and experiences. Such relationships can create social anxieties as well as social judgements that may conceal unacknowledged envy or hostility. Some men find it difficult to have satisfying and trusting relationships with other men; they may find relationships with women can be enjoyable and less complicated. Where no significant relationships exist, we may gain solace from imagined or fantasy relationships.

MARRIAGE AND FRIENDSHIP

In the years of our youth, many of us moved, sometimes hurriedly, into marriage. It appeared to settle the anxieties and uncertainties of the male-female relationships, and often sealed off any further exploration of intimate relationships. At that time, some went on holidays with other couples, were open to larger dinner parties, or joined sporting and church groups, political parties and other social groups. All of these activities gave acceptable expression to the varieties of mingling with males and females and exploring the intellectual, social, and emotional enjoyment and stimulation that friendships bring.

As marriages now last much longer, they can become marred by a series of disappointments and difficulties. Whereas the initial idealisation of the couple may have held many anticipated pleasures, it also brought many unappeased resentments, realities that contributed to unresolved conflicts. A woman may say, 'My husband was such a terrible father. That's what made him into what he was!' A man may say, 'I never realised until later years that my wife's constant anger arose out of her inferiority. Try as we did, nothing could shift this deep-seated belief that she was always unfavourably compared with her talented sister. I, too, was at fault for marrying her. Another man could have brought her the happiness that I could never provide'.

There is a view that some marriages cannot be sustained, that realities should be faced, and the two people go their separate ways. Most will recognise that such a 'solution' has many difficulties. It would involve complex financial arrangements, balancing relationships with adult children, and gaining a new identity and a different sense of belonging.

Relationship Rewards

1. Provide a satisfying awareness of one's acceptance, affirmation and likeability to people across conventional boundaries.
2. Provide helpfulness and support in times of particular need.
3. Provide a sense of security in telling one's story.
4. Provide a sense of critical reality in the quest for authenticity in a relationship.
5. Provide a joining of memories of the past, a common optimism about the future, and a sense of continuity and meaning over time.
6. Provide some scope for playfulness, expansiveness and enjoyment.
7. Provide a non-possessive openness in shared relationships.

GRIEVING FRIENDSHIPS

Friendships change. An event may occur, causing one party to question the integrity of the other. Even after decades of a friendship, an apparently minor conflict may be sufficient to provoke one party to end the friendship. The rupture may have arisen from conflict, from personality sensitivities, or from a loss of resilience in the relationship. One party may declare that they can never forgive or forget what occurred. The other feels relieved that they are free of the obligations and implications of the friendship.

The loss of a friendship may affect other relationships. It can provoke despondency, and emotions of anger and resentment. It can result in feelings of guilt and hopelessness, a loss of self-esteem, and even self-compassion. It can deeply affect who we perceive ourselves to be. Much will depend on the kind of friendship and the part that the other person played in our lives. The ability to adapt will depend on our personality, expansiveness and resilience, and transcendence. A number of evaluations may be made:

Evaluating Friendships

1. What event(s) has caused the conflict or rupture?
2. What significance and meaning are given to the event? Is its importance categorical? Or can it be softened or negotiated?

3. What emotional loading has been vested on the event? Can these emotions be curtailed or reduced?
4. Who are the interested parties? And are they accessible and amenable to change?
5. What are the priorities of healing the rupture? What resources and agencies are available? What are the costs and consequences of the rupture compared with the benefits of restoration?
6. Is the person open to the choices and actions involved in restoration?

The role of spirituality in finding meaning and contentment was the focus in this chapter. I now make a shift to the ways we can soothe the emotional pain of death. How the death of a loved one brings with it the unavoidable acceptance of the death and the necessity of containing the emotions that become part of it. The experiences, stages, and processes involved in adapting to the new reality are discussed. Practical ways to celebrate and honour a life, plan a good funeral, and give a meaningful eulogy, are given.

AGEING WELL

Chapter 4

A Good Life Deserves a Good Ending

Our daily newspapers bring news of many tragedies. A mother aged 34 died trying to save her husband from drowning. Innocent people are run down in the street as they go about their everyday lives. At any one time thousands will experience the death of an intimate partner. If we take account of this possibility that with every one of these deaths, at least three people are intimately affected, on top of that extended family members and whole communities are affected. That is a huge number of people trying to adapt, recover, and remake their lives after one death.

Often death is anticipated, because we knew

the person was dying. But, death itself is a lonely time: only we can do our dying. Some have a terrible hell of a life and a terrible death. They may say 'Thank God it's over'. They may hasten it to avoid further pain. Others will say, 'It was a good life, why not also a good death?' 'I am grateful for the life I had and grateful that I could do something to make it better for myself and others.'

Perhaps this is the hope and the 'blessing' expressed in the obituaries that state 'they died peacefully', 'they died a good death', 'they died surrounded by their family'. Whereas in the past ageing was seen in the negative perspective of decline, the suggested alternative could see the last years as phases of growth towards the culmination of life in a welcomed, easy death. There is some soundness therefore in St Paul's words (though literalism stretches the point too far) when he wrote 'Death, where is your sting. Grave where is your victory?' The poet Dylan Thomas exhorted his dying father to meet his death as something to be confronted, rather than something that was helplessly accepted. He did this by urging him not to go gently into that good night. But rather he encouraged him to rage, rage, against the dying of the light.

LIFE AFTER LOSS

Feelings of remorse, guilt, regret, and going over what could or might have been, are common following the death of a significant person in our life. This occurs no matter what their age, or their relationship with us. Identifying the pathways that are realistic possibilities for reshaping a new and different personal existence becomes a necessary goal. If that is not done, the loss of a significant relationship, such as a husband, wife or partner, becomes a double loss.

Remorse and regret can hold us in a regressed posture, when what is required is a comprehensive release. That release does not necessarily mean shaping a readiness for another relationship. It means re-shaping our existence in the most enjoyable and releasing way possible. The person may find this process difficult, and professional help might be considered.

First to give access to an adequate grieving, second to provide a process to reshape existence into the future, and third to resolve the ego strength that will be necessary for the release and reshaping to take place. The end of the partnership brings the need to confront the deep sense of emptiness and loneliness after years of sharing a home and many life events. The insidious resentment that the surviving partner is left to make the necessary post-death arrangements needs to be addressed.

As well as addressing the necessary social expectations associated with bereavement, there is the anxiety pervading many uncertainties. For some, their partner was helper, friend, confidante, sounding board, comforter, partner in the business of living, protector of privacies, cover for personal and social shortcomings and failures, a carrier of compassion, a co-parent guiding the next generation, a softening, strengthening presence.

HEALING AFTER THE DEATH OF A LOVED ONE

Death of a partner or spouse at any age brings with it the unavoidable necessity of acceptance of the death, the simultaneous and the continuing necessity of containing the emotions that become part of it. It brings with it the necessity of adapting to the loss, and the necessity of reshaping and reconstructing existence in the weeks after the loss. Elsewhere, I have written about the phases of death and dying, how we might experience them, anticipate them, and move through them. At any time, we can experience the following emotions at any time alone, or all at once.

Shock and Numbness

This is the phase where there is a sense that the loss is not real and thus it seems impossible to accept. There is physical distress during this phase, which can result in somatic symptoms. If we do not progress through this phase, we will struggle to accept and understand our emotions and communicate them. We will shut down emotionally and not progress through the phases of grief.

Yearning and Searching

In this phase we are acutely aware of the void in our life from the loss. The future we imagined is no longer a possibility. We search for the comfort we used to have from the person we have lost, and we try to fill the void of their absence. We may appear preoccupied with the person. We continue identifying with the person who has died, looking for constant reminders of them, and ways to be close to them. If we cannot progress through this phase, we will spend our remaining life trying to fill the void, and will remain preoccupied with the person we have lost.

Despair and Disorganisation

Here, we have accepted that everything has changed and it will not go back to the way it was or the way we imagined. There is a hopelessness and despair that come with this, as well as anger and questioning. Life feels as though it will never improve or make sense again without the presence of the person who died. We may withdraw from others. It has been argued that if we do not progress through this phase we will continue to be consumed by anger and depression, our attitude toward life will remain negative and hopeless.

Reorganising and Recovering

While in this phase, our faith in life starts to be restored. We establish new goals and patterns of day-to-day life. Slowly we start to rebuild and come to realise our life can still be positive, even after the loss. Our trust is slowly restored. In this phase our grief does not go away nor is it fully resolved. The loss recedes and shifts to a hidden section of the brain. There, it continues to influence us, but it is not at the forefront of the mind.

MOVING ON

Some deaths bring relief to the surviving partner. 'She suffered too long. Death was merciful at the finish. Our marriage did not turn out as we had hoped. They will say, but we made our vows, "til death us do part", and so we did not even pretend that another life would be possible.' 'When he died, it was a great release. I was able to be a free woman, as I had never known before. No, I would certainly not marry again. But I was able to build a different life with many men and women friends. I was never able to do that when I was married and he was alive. I always had to say where I was going and with whom. Now I am free to come and go as I like.'

Others might say, 'For 48 years I lived a very tidy married life. I thought I was happy, but now I know that all these years were like living under a kind of criticism every day. And everybody 'out there' thought we were a happily married couple. He has been dead five years. Now and again I wonder what he would have done if I had died first. I don't think he would have coped; but who knows? The fact remains — two people wasted their lives in a relationship that neither of us enjoyed, but our religion, or our stupidity, kept us in that dazed state until he died!'

QUIETING RESPONSES AND SELF-SOOTHING

Most of us hope there will be some quietness and soothing for the distress associated with our many losses. When we have suffered a physical injury, we know that there is a sense of soothing flowing from others. All that may flow from others carries sensitivities, too many or too few, or what is appropriate and acceptable, or what is totally private. Attempts to soothe may make matters worse. Much will depend on relationships, perceptions, past experiences, and interpretations and meanings. Many will assert that their needs of soothing are essentially interpersonal. These needs may become a demand, an expectation, and a statement of social importance.

While we may find temporary relief, others may not find any relief, not least because they may believe that relief is not possible. The dimensions of the disruption are so extensive in size and direction, that they realise they might need to learn some ways to live with their persisting emotional pain, and learn ways to achieve and transcend these emotions. The emotional pain may be manifested in or exacerbated by anxious and irrational thinking. It can involve churning over what might have been, compulsive and obsessive preoccupations, uncontrolled memories and emotions, disruptive behaviours, and the loss of enjoyment in relationships.

SOOTHING EMOTIONAL PAIN

In some cases, such as the death of a loved one, the emotional pain can be so severe and extensive that it is understandable that we would yearn for an effective soothing that would flow to us from a reliable external source. Distress may be manifested in the interpretation of the experience, in the memory of what occurred, in behaviour that is destructive and demoralising. It can result in an inability to contain emotional distress, in the disruption of relationships, and in a loss of self-strengths. Although distressing experiences may carry severe and prolonged mental and emotional pain, and personal disruption, the impact on the sufferer and the focus of emotional pain have many differences.

As such, the focus of the intervention and the relief that follows will have many differences. Often, however, we are faced with the reality that we will need to do our soothing within ourselves. In the face of intense emotional distress, we lose the capacity to self-soothe. We may become aware that we never had the capacity, or we refuse to face the deficit in our ability to regulate our emotions. As we recognise the benefits that can flow from emotional soothing, our search to find that soothing will increase. Soothing brings quietness to mind, emotions, behaviour, and our troubled relationships. Soothing may be a broad-brush approach evoking a general sensation of being soothed. Alternatively, it can be specifically focused on mind, emotions, behaviour or relationships. It can become a vital tool in our quest to age successfully.

Principles of Self-Soothing

1. Softening of the painful reality.
2. Searching for a reduction of the emotional pain.
3. Supportive strengths.
4. Self-strengths.
5. Soothing words are spoken.
6. Stabilise emotions.
7. Openness to healing and soothing.
8. Surround the hurt zone with softening influences and distractions.

ADAPTING TO THE NEW REALITY

The grieving person draws some comfort from the assurance that their father is now at rest with their mother; that a child is now an angel in heaven. Others propose to erect a memorial by which their loved one will be remembered. In some instances a family is relieved that their suffering is over. Though their grief is painful in the deepest emotional way, there is comfort that the pain will pass. The reality is stark. The person who was once a present reality has gone. And life must go on without them. Everyone who knows the reality of loss also knows that a new reality awaits them: a life without the person now dead. We hear people say 'we get by; its tough, but we will get through this'. But is there a better way?

Whenever death occurs there is the real possibility of becoming overwhelmed by grief, held in the powerful zone of loss and emptiness, and we find, or stumble to find, a way to live in this new reality. Grief, and our attachment to the now gone, may begin to define our reality of loss — or it may open up a different reality — a finding or stumbling into the resilience to live more positively, creatively, appreciating its sense of renewal.

A GOOD FUNERAL

A good life deserves a good funeral. What is a good funeral? You have heard people say, 'We gave her a good send-off'. What made it a 'good' send off? I have attended funerals commemorating the lives of people I knew across some 80 years. I have said many times — a person who has lived a very short life, and a person who has lived 98 years should each have a good funeral. Some addresses have lacked the gravitas such occasions merit. Funerals can be inspiring and memorable, and they can be long and laboured.

People are reticent in talking about their own funeral, yet it is common to hear some say what they do not want — 'I don't want any speeches, any music, any flowers'. Some feel they are not worth a good funeral; they quietly hope that a few might attend, but there is an apprehension that nobody will. While they acknowledge that it does not matter after their death, we know that deep down it does matter! Although the deceased person is no longer present, the family in their mourning might act as if the deceased person is present.

Generally, there are four types of public funerals. The deceased person has had a religious affiliation, and so their funeral would contain the appropriate religious content. Some had no religious belonging. They may have left instructions that there should be no religious content. But families might assume that funerals are 'meant' to have some religious reference, and a selected clergy will impose a religious content on the funeral. At other funerals where overt religious reference is avoided, speakers provide readings and commentary that reflect the ways in which the life of the person gave meaning and significance to individual lives or to life in general.

HOW TO PLAN A CELEBRATION OF LIFE

Planning the celebration of the life of a person whom we have loved, or been involved with, is really a process of asking and answering a number of questions. It requires us to sit down with family members, at least once, to explore ideas for the celebration. Ideas will arise from answering the following questions.

1. Who will be invited? The number of guests define the where, when and how of your celebration of life. Write down the names of everyone you think would want to be there and

then set it aside. You can add new names to the list as you go along.

2. Where and when, should the event take place? Here is where your imagination must be tempered by any scheduling or travel related issues facing those to be invited. Be sure to contact out-of-town relatives and friends about their situation before settling on these critical details.

3. Who will orchestrate or conduct the event? If your loved one was religious, you may opt to have their past or present church minister perform these tasks. However, many families today hire a non-denominational celebrant to oversee the celebration of life.

4. Who wishes to speak at the event? Many times family members or friends will be very direct about their desire to make a short presentation at the celebration of life. When this does not apply you need to ask if they would be willing to publicly share their thoughts and feelings. Either way, you'll want to select those people who have shared a close relationship with the deceased and have something meaningful to contribute.

5. What group activities would be appropriate? We've heard some exciting celebration of life ideas over the years. This question involves thinking about what your loved one liked most about their life. It gives everyone a remarkable space to share memories, laugh, and even cry together.

6. What food or beverages should be served? What you serve may depend on the theme of your celebration of life, or it may be based on your loved one's favourite dishes. It's entirely up to you: we've even seen 'pot luck' celebrations of life where guests actually sign up to bring select foods and beverages.

7. What readings and music should you include? Music is an integral part of life for many people, and a celebration of life is the perfect event in which to showcase the meaningful music of your loved one. But, if your loved one didn't appreciate music (and many do not), it may be more appropriate to read chosen spiritual selections, or excerpts from literature.

8. What details of your loved one's life do you want to share with guests? A recitation of every

biographical detail may be tiresome! Sometimes you can reveal their character most effectively by detailing one short moment in their life.

9. What technology will you use? Many families create a tribute video and use it as the centrepiece of the event. Others choose to use a memory table of photographs and other memorabilia.

HOW TO GIVE A GOOD EULOGY

Farewells are probably more satisfying if spoken when the person is alive and is able to appreciate what is being said, but few people are able to do these 'final things', and so they are deferred until it is then too late. You may have heard, or read, where a dying parent has called her children to her deathbed and said some final words to each one, but this is probably rarely done. Parting emotions can be very distressing, and may well be unpredictable.

At the funeral, family members will usually give eulogies as if the deceased is 'somewhere up there listening'. They might make a confession that they might not have acted as they feel they should have, and they will say their sorrowful last good-bye to a mother or father. If the parent has been lost in dementia for several years, the words addressed to the deceased are likely to be doubly painful.

Families are often disappointed that the people they invited to give a tribute at the funeral make a mess of it. Did this happen because they did not know how to give a tribute, or did they fail to focus on those aspects the family thought should be emphasised? The last public words uttered on a person's life should be words that not only honour the person who has lived and died, but lift and expand the humanity of all who hear.

People occasionally ask me, 'Where do you go to church?' After half a century of trying to develop the art of relevant preaching, it is a question I usually leave unanswered, except for those occasions when the experience has been a notable inspiration. Such an occasion came my way recently when my search threw onto my computer the eulogy for Senator John McCain delivered by President Barack Obama. I have heard scores of eulogies and tributes. Many of them are memorable because they were done so badly. If you want to know how to give a good eulogy listen to Barack Obama. The days of truly good public speaking are not over.

A LETTER TO A GRIEVING WOMAN

It is often said that we do not know what to say when someone dies. No matter the age, stage, or the way the person died, we can feel lost for words or left searching for the appropriate thing to say. As such, we refrain from saying anything at all, believing this the most appropriate path to follow.

Yet we know words comfort, encourage and support, no matter how the death occurred. Words affirm the life of the person who has died, provide comfort to those who loved them, and they acknowledge the life that has been lived. An example of the words that might encourage and support a woman might be as follows.

'I hope the funeral brought you a strong sense of pride and goodness. Through it all, there was sadness and also inspiration. It was a time to recall many memories, and it was a time to connect with many sources of healing.'

'All the speakers at the funeral were memorable, because they spoke so well. I reflected that from early years, a young man had grown into full maturity and became a model and inspiration for his own, and his wider family, and to the several communities he joined.'

'His father died when he was still a boy, just

10 years old. His mother became a sole parent, a working mother, a model of courage. With slender resources, she became that source of unconditional support for her three sons. She drew a great deal of that courage and her values from her mother who always was mother, friend, and close confidant.

'You, his wife, carried and conveyed that same character and these same good values. The women of the world play a large part in fashioning and strengthening and softening the lives of their men. You have clearly been a strong presence in that line of influences and goodness.'

'The dying time is a deeply painful time; and so is the time of grieving, loss, and loneliness. The funeral brought together a large number of people who, on such a day, were warmly united in their support and care for you. The days ahead will be different, that support and care will fade, as these caring people turn to attend to their own cares.'

'Although some will say, "time will heal", those who most feel the pain of loss, know that they need something more to be in place, as time does its healing.'

'Kindness and strength — sometimes from unexpected places — will augment the kindness and strength you discover that has quietly grown within you. As you find the gift of that kindness and strength, you will see that it becomes part of the gift that you bring to others.'

Above I described how we all search for a greater spiritual awareness, of the rituals, the experiences, and the relationships, that give life meaning. Next, I write of our persistent hunger for a new depth of spirituality. Included are meditations, prayers, and my interpretations of the scriptures. I trust it might assist in your own search for meaning, and keep alive your persisting existential hunger.

Chapter 5

Meditations, Prayers and Scriptures

Our meditations and prayers are an expression of hope. They are that aspiration that through all the exigencies of life, we might reach out to be in harmony with a higher energy, a good presence, with that spiritual universe that we strive to understand. They are an expression of wonder at the astonishing aspects of life and our profound gratitude and amazement that for a time, we have had a part in it, and hopefully, contribute to its colour and goodness, and the health and wellbeing of the world.

MEDITATIONS

Sunrise

Walk in the quietness. Hear your footsteps. Breathe the stillness. Pause amongst ordinary things and be alive to special places.

May the coming of the morning remind you that each day you rise again. Let the trees bring a message from those who planted them here. Let the gardens carry smells and colours of a living world.

May the running water stir memories of life-giving waters in many places. Feel a growing harmony with light and shadow, with silence and sound, with inner quietness and outer spaces.

May your soul be enriched and expanded by the soul of the world. Let the present moment be the time to follow your bliss.

A Good Spirit

There is a Good Spirit in the world and we would be in harmony with it. We reach out to the best, as it has been in the past, as it has been and is in other places, so may the best be our present desire.

We will act wisely to provide food and water and clean air on the planet. We will act wisely to care for all that is below the surface of this Earth and all that stretches into the galaxies.

We aim to rise above violence and destruction and hate, all ugly behaviour, all malevolent thoughts. We will celebrate everything good, everything beautiful, everything worthy of praise.

Streams of Consciousness

Insignificant frightened and alone I breathe the wind of the stars
And am carried beyond my hiding place.
I feel the winds of God lifting me to be a citizen of the world,
guardian of the cosmos, discovering the gift and power of the New Creation.
In this boat of fragile life on uncertain seas, ambient intermittent darkness, we strain to see through the winds of the storm
And hear that Voice of hope of one and everyone who dares to say
It is I.
Do not be afraid… and the boat finds its haven and its peace.
And so the stream of life, flows around us beneath us and over us, being and non-being
Of water, wind, noise, and people and pathways in the sky
And I lifted by the streams of new life to a new consciousness of who I am

And what this life can be, of kingdoms here, and the kingdom which we pray will come.
And I a worker, a leader, a follower, a healer, a prophet, a buyer, a seller with power of mind and heart, of pen, and voice, of commerce and computer, and heights and all the rush of day by day.
A victim of our dreams or others' dreams, and minds and eyes tunnelled, turned and glazed
Until we, here then there, hear again the word, lift up your heads — behold how beautiful are the feet of him who brings good tidings.
A new consciousness of who we are and what we — our children — will become.
Break forth together in shouts of triumph, you who have longed for that liberation.

A Land of Fire and Floods

We live in a land of fire, of floods, of long droughts and bountiful harvests. We live in times of great affluence and times of severe loss. We are part of a people of vast knowledge and know-how and a people deeply dependent on the resources of the Earth and its people.

From the painful landscapes of ash and rubble new life will flourish. In the days and months of sadness and sorrow may new strength be found. From the chaos and catastrophe a thoughtful attitude will be developed.

From the abundant generosity of so many may new communities find a new identity. From the vast goodwill of talk and travail may we all know the healing power of the human soul.

A Self Reflection

May we live our life with gratitude, compassion, expansiveness and with an enriching happiness. May we in our own lives live with goodwill and grace, with harmony and hope.

May we see good reason to celebrate the past. May we with good compassion and courage confront the pains we carry. May we with a strong spirit continue to believe in the great possibilities waiting in the future.

May we pause to wonder that human beings in all their difference and impatience can find empathy for each other and a sympathy for all human sorrow and pain. May we quietly wait for that desired transformation of our inner spirit.

May we here remember with gratitude times and places and people that will always be important to us. May we keep alive our belief that along with every achievement and activity, and every step we take, we honour the gifts of life, creativity and growth.

Mindfulness

May we find a pathway through our old resentments and our ongoing renewals. Being released from those things that diminish us, may we build into our lives those things that enlarge and enrich us.

Where we can be a good influence even in a small way, help us to be it. Where we can be an encouragement and a comfort to someone, help us to do it.

Where we can make a contribution to some worthwhile cause, help us to begin the task and help us to sustain the desire.

Where we can help the children to grow into good human beings, help us to be active in those vital processes and in those important environments.

Intimacy

We know we can be separate and close. We have taken many pathways in our life but today we want to find and focus on the pathway that will be best for us. May all our good memories carry us toward a new meaning for our life.

May all our good thoughts and our various tasks be held together by a good strength that runs through our life. And we are grateful for a good place to be, people who bring goodness to our life, the pathways we are now on, possibilities that open before us the pleasures that bring some lightness to the dark patches of life.

The Magic of Autumn

Don't miss the magic of Autumn, the shades of green, the iridescent orange, the restful brown, the rustle of the leaves in the breeze, the sound of walking feet. Don't miss the magic of Autumn, the leaves and God of the light, God of all colour and God of precious sight, God of things dying, God of vanishing things and God of things inspiring new life.

Let our whole being be alert and alive lest we miss the magic and the gift to Autumn. Let the beauty of things outweigh the ugliness of things. Let the kindness and compassion of human beings outweigh the hurts and hates of human beings. Let our whole being find a vital comfort and consolation, lest we miss the gift of life's continuing goodness.

God of Faith that brings good gifts, that will help us embrace the gifts of life more than the deficits of life, that will help us embrace the beauty of life more than the barbs of life, that will help us embrace the magic of a changing autumn in the world outside and the moments of a changing autumn in our inner world.

Bliss

May you walk the unused track, and your eyes widen as you see the spider's web stretched across the path glistening in the early dew. May you find a way through the forest and hear the noise and songs of many birds, and your heart leap to the swift flight of the crimson rosellas.

May you walk your favourite beach and watch the waves roll incessantly over the sand. May you stand high on the headland and hear the distant call of the plover.

May you pause to hear the wind softly blowing through the long grass. May you look far into the horizon and to the changing blue of the mountain ranges.

May you turn and feel the gentle warmth of the rising sun on your back. May you know you experience a special moment of life, your soul expanded, and your spirit consumed in Bliss.

Listen

Listen to the way you speak
Listen to the way you walk
Listen to the way you breathe
Listen to your moods
Listen to someone saying something beautiful
to you

Listen to the music you understand and to the music you cannot understand
Listen to another language
Listen to what someone is saying with their eyes
Listen to the wind in the trees
Listen to the rain
Listen to the rolling of the ocean and to the stillness of peaceful waters
Listen to that bird that has not yet begun its morning song
Listen to the silence
Listen to the softness of the stars
Listen to your clasped hands
Listen to a consoling presence
Listen to your best self
Listen to the future that calls you
Listen...Listen again...Listen

Take Time

Take time to be still — it brings a new quietness to your mind and body. Take time to clear your mind and body of negative emotions — it is a way to a higher sense of well-being.

Take time to study the possible consequences of your behaviour — it could help you avoid much pain and it could save others much pain.

Take time to let go the distressing memories and

the pain of past times — it will begin to release you for a happier healthier future.

Take time to be realistically optimistic — it will help you cope better, you will feel better, and you will be better company with others. Take time to recognise the things that will bring you joy and laughter — it will enrich your life and the life of others.

Take time to ask the question: What is the road, now, that I will travel? It will help you focus on the direction your life will take, and the baggage you will carry. Take time to ponder: What is it deep down that I really, really want? It will help you decide deep, deep down, whether you will really seek what you say you (really deep down) want.

Take time to speak of deeper things to your friend — it will make a huge difference to the way you live in the world. Take time to listen to great wisdom — it lifts you to a wider awareness of your place in time.

Take time to wait on a strength beyond your own — it is a stream of healing power. Take time to ponder the unsolvable eternal mysteries of life — it will bring you closer to a sense of awe and wonder and to what is common in all humanity.

Sounds and Echoes of Beauty

May you see in so many things that are old the signs and sensations of real beauty. May you be open to see in things that are completely new the surprise of something of real beauty.

May you pause to hold in your mind some memories of times and people and places of great beauty. May you be ready to be softened and healed, enhanced and excited by the little things of beauty.

May you be ready to listen to things of beauty, taste and touch things of beauty, see and smell things of beauty. May you desire beauty, create beauty, and bestow beauty. May you radiate beauty to others and to the world.

PRAYERS

A Prayer of Comfort and Courage

Eternal Spirit, let the spirit of comfort and courage give new hope to all who today remember the pains of war.

Eternal Spirit, let the spirit of goodness transform the spirits of all who today continue to beat-out the destruction of war.

Eternal Spirit, let the spirit of healing bring a

quietening healing to our spirits:
let us be a support to all who are unsteady
let us be a good presence to all who mourn
let us be a source of inspiration to all who have lost sight of their best pathway in life.

A Prayer for a New Year

We move to a new year, a new phase of our life, a new challenge at work, a new era in our relationships, a new wave in world affairs.

We pause:

There is gratitude for the good experiences that came our way in the year now past

There is hope for healing of the wounds and the scars we carry

There is the anxiety we remember, and through that there is a searching for good things yet to unfold

There is the courage we found to meet the unexpected

There was the celebration of the times and gifts of happiness, contentment and energy

To remember the little things we almost failed to notice, but then we saw how special — even sacred — they were

The big things that nearly overwhelmed us and would have convinced us gloom was the only way to live. We discovered new eyes to see things differently. We found a new heart that suddenly overflowed with generosity.

Remind Us:

of the good energy life gives us every day

of the best feelings and emotions that can be ours every day

of the joyful moments and moods that can be turning points for us every day.

Bring:

comfort to the world of suffering people

hope to the world of poverty and hunger

peace to the world of hostility and war

gratitude and generosity to the world of plenty.

Spirit of Life:

let there be a harmony in our spirits

lift us out of our daily state of busyness to a state of quietness

lift us out of our unsettled mind to find some moments of serenity

lift us out of our fragmented thoughts to focus on what is of deepest importance to us at this time.

Help Us:

to become part of a good energy in life

to encourage and endorse a goodness of heart and soul

to be enlarged and enhanced as we contemplate the amazing gifts of life.

to become part of a better humanity as we are open to people of different cultures and colour, race and religion, values and viewpoints.

A Prayer of Inspiration

Good Presence in all the events and experiences of every day:

may our inner self be open to the flow of new energy

may our inner self be ready to wait for good things to occur

may our inner self be conscious of a connection with a new harmony

may our inner self find quietness, and strength and its important healing.

God of the Good Presence:

may we see something of your presence in the eyes of people we meet may we see something of your presence in the generosity of one to another

may we see something of your presence as we join others in stepping over cynicism and become a circle of celebration

may we see something of your presence in the process

of justice and the words of compassion.

Good Spirit of God:

may all who feel their spirits are low, or somewhat lost behind the many veils of life, feel the renewing and releasing presence of God's Good Spirit

may all who look for new strength be open to the strength of the Spirit of Life

may all who are in the midst of sorrow feel the veil of sadness lifted, as life calls to life, as hope strengthens hope.

God of the Good Presence all around us:

release us from our limiting attitudes and circumstances, that we may rise to bring some fresh goodness to each new day

open us to positive ways to cope with the difficulties of life. Turn us around to celebrate the simple joys of life

remind us each day of the astonishing gifts of old

friendships and new beginnings; of pathways well-trodden, and new possibilities waiting for us to explore

restore in us a good energy and a good spirit for each day.

A Prayer of Affirmation

In this prayer focus on the Good Presence within you, a Good Presence in yourself, a Good Presence strong enough to reduce the power and the hold of your recurring negativity and anxiety.

May the Good Presence grow within us, and — transform our way of seeing things; transform our way of relating to others; transform the kind of people we can be.

We pause to give thanks for the Gift of Life. The gift of new life, the gift of good influences of life, the gift of hope that life will continue to bring its healing and goodness — after times anxiety and sadness.

We pause to give thanks that life surrounds us with people who can bring new meaning to our life, good memories that will ever enrich our Life, good supports that hold us in focus in different ways.

God of the Gift, God of the Good Presence may we take the gift, may we take the Good Presence and walk with others, talk with others and together, celebrate the Gift and together, ever search for the Good Presence in all life.

May goodwill be generously spread along our pathway, may goodwill flow generously from our hearts. May goodwill be the high priority of the world.

A Prayer of Reflection

In this prayer we reflect quietly on our life — and our desire for a balance of healing and hope — healing for our lost self-image and hope for renewed energy of our ideals. In this prayer we wait for good moments that will re-establish the courage we need, and that will give us a new faith to live each day.

May the God and Spirit of caring and compassion keep us connected, even when we tear ourselves away. May the God and Spirit of Comfort and Consolation be real to all who feel the ache of life's alienation and anxiety.

May the God and Spirit of Life's Best memories keep calling us to live life at its Best. May the God who gives us the gift of Life give us also a double portion of Gratitude and Goodwill.

May we find the pathway to the Good and the Tender and the Beautiful, and live each day to affirm our place on that pathway.

A Prayer for Peace

Eternal God, we look beyond the circumstances of our life to find some beauty, peace and grace. Point us again to those places where we will find something beautiful.

Confirm in us the belief that peace and goodwill are better than conflict and destruction. And help us all to see again the meaning of grace in life. In the very centre of our body we search for a sense of strength and harmony.

In the many expressions of our personality we search for the best person we can be. We pause to listen to that Higher Spirit to renew our spirit. Where we grieve, may the Good Presence hold us for another day and carry us forward. Where we are frustrated and angry, God open our blocked lifelines.

God of this new day if our dreams have lost their colour help us to put new colours into our dreams. If our pathways have become blocked, let some help come to us to roll those blocks away that we might find new spaces opening up for us. If we have come to take life for granted, lift us into a new spirit of generosity and gratitude for life's challenges and life's joys.

A Prayer of Hope

May we recognise each new day that as the sun rises, new energy floods our part of the world. May we — even in our shadows of pain and sorrow, find the strength to help us live with a faith that carries us forward.

Help us onto pathways that will lead us to a new state of mind and heart. Help us to loosen the pain of our catastrophes and crucifixions that we may rise to embrace our restoration and resurrection.

Help us to loosen the grip of fear in our lives and in our society, that we will tap into the resources of courage and hope, reach out to new possibilities for ourselves, and a more positive vision of our world.

Help us to loosen the power of the worrisome past, the powers of a worrying future that we might live with a positive strength and inspiration in the present. Help us to be part of all goodness, all beauty and the fullest satisfaction of what is possible.

A Prayer of Gratitude

We pause with gratitude as we reflect on the larger pathway of our life and also on the everyday experiences. We are grateful for the capacity to step through difficult times and we are grateful for the experience of many satisfactions and times of celebration.

We give thanks for the gift of our inner energy, for many strengths and good sensitivities, for intelligence and inspiration, for positive beliefs, and a helpful religion.

And so our gratitude is our strong response to the gifts of life. Each day comes with its tasks and difficulties. And the contemplation of the longer-term future is coloured by uncertainty and anxiety — times of waiting and times of worry.

May we find the right courage to cope; the right patience to persist; and the right mind and mood to make the moments mean more.

A Prayer for Energy

In spite of so much that can be depressing and demanding, keep alive our energy of hope. Every day we need hope in small packets and large bundles; and when all hope has dwindled away, help us to reconnect with the energy of faith that opens up a pathway for us to take. Give a bundle of hope and a pathway of faith to each one facing difficult and draining times.

May we be open to be a caring and healing community. May we bring to our work and world a nourished and nurturing spirit. May we be carriers of hope, carriers of tolerance, carriers of courage, carriers of beliefs in new ways to cope with our stresses and strains. May our faith be renewed in ourselves, in people, in the future, in a power and energy beyond us that strengthens our faith.

A Prayer for Inspiration

We are grateful for our life, for strength and courage to meet the challenges and the sorrows, for inspiration and renewal of happiness that come in many forms, for health of body, health of mind and health of spirit.

With our gifts, our abilities, our energy, we bring new focus to the future — the things we have to do, the things we would like to do, and the things we must prepare to do: in our work, in our career, in preparing for the ages and stages of life. Help us to keep alive the energy of hope and optimism and good intentions.

May our care and concern reach out to larger horizons beyond ourselves: to people facing difficult and anxious times; to the world calling for more people to stand up for justice, human rights, and human goodness; for our planet, the home of people, the place of all wild life, the airways and waterways that give life to all living creatures; for the vital work of protection, nourishment and growth.

A Prayer for Courage

The moments of time are quickly filled with frustration and resentment over what is lost. Every moment of goodness is to be welcomed and worshipped. Every moment can be a moment of quietness, a moment of listening, a moment of self healing, a moment of hope.

Help us to find courage in all moments of life, there is courage in this moment, there is some joy in this moment, there is gratitude in this moment. Help us to find joy in our moments of life, something good to remember, something good to celebrate, something good to carry into the next moment.

May our moments of ugliness be transformed by our moments of goodness. May our moments of scepticism be transformed by moments of an expansive faith. May our moments when our tides run low be transformed by the flood of new life, new energy and new hope.

Whenever we are dominated by the urgency of time, may we savour the moment that is ours. Whenever we are aware the time is running out, may we embrace the moment that is ours. Whenever we realise we left destruction in our past moment, may we realise our next moment invites us to recognise it is a new moment. May we discover in the silent moment some new strength, and that we may hear in the noisy stressful moment, some new awareness of the great gift of every moment.

A Prayer for Energy and Strength

God the energy of all creation, around us — each one of us is unique in our thoughts, in our feelings, in our response to the past, in our dreams and hopes for the future.

There is uniqueness in our different strengths. There is uniqueness in our differing vulnerabilities. Our life is lived behind a thin protective shield every day. And every day we need that protective shield to be strengthened.

There are times when all our protective strengths come under testing. There are times when some of our protective strengths are not strong enough.

In those times we are grateful that new strengths come from various sources. Help each one of us to develop the protections we need.

Help us all to be grateful for the strengths we are given and the strengths which are there for us, and the strengths imparted by others.

May we recognise and use wisely and well our strengths and may we realise how wisely and well we can be a strength to others.

A Prayer for Mindful Living

God of all Creation, in the mysterious and beautiful balance of life, one part depends on another, one part protects the other, and all of life continues under a fragile and vital protective shield.

Help us to correct our own destructiveness.

Help us to protect the vital balance of things.

Help us to value the very gift of life.

Help us to embrace life as fully as we can, to enjoy it and share it as far as we can.

Help us to respect the life of others.

The task of our life is to embrace the best spirit, to be carriers of the best wisdom, to live out the most generous emotions. May all that is ahead of us draw us more fully into this task.

A Prayer for Humanity

We pause in considerable awe as we reflect on the complex richness of our emotions. Often these feelings get confused, get tangled in conflict, giving us many complications.

We are often enlarged by the emotions of joy and happiness, of generosity and care, and we are often capsized by emotions of anger and rage, of fear and hate. We know that all humanity is enriched as we persistently practise our positive emotions.

We know that our relationships are enriched as we hold onto the hope of harmony. We know that all spirits are strengthened and our health is lifted as we show care and concern, as we speak words of encouragement and kindness.

May we continually search to be in touch with the source of all that is Good and Positive and Beautiful.

A Prayer for the Grieving

Send a good restoring thought to those who grieve. Send some good courage to those who are facing difficult anxieties in their life.

Send that strengthening resilience to those who know the times of being at their worst, that they may re-find pathways to the best strength and best hope.

Let no dark moments prevent us from seeing the light of a new day. Let no grief keep us from embracing the good things life continues to unfold for us. Let no anxiety block the strength that surrounds us and flows into our spirit.

Help us to listen and grow, play, and laugh, be restored and renewed, each day.

A Prayer of Hope

There are times when we feel drained — drained of good energy, drained of good intentions, drained of good feelings.

But when our cup is full, we are ready to live again. When our cup is full, we know the joy of being alive. We pause for our cup to be filled again.

We know what it feels like when someone brings a good word to us — it is like filling up the cup of happiness. Help us then to bring some happiness and affirmation, some good word to others, that their cup will be full.

A Prayer for Everyday Troubles

Every day comes with its troubles. Every day has a carryover from yesterday. Every day has an anxiety about tomorrow. Every day is every person's challenge. Every day comes with the gift of expectation and hope.

Good Spirit of God may we be open to the right wisdom, to deal with life's many problems, may we be open to the right mood of expectation and hope.

Give a thought to people who are not coping with life — to people who have been injured and cannot return to work and have lost faith in the system: to people who gave support to good causes, but have lost faith in people.

Give a thought to people who have so many problems they have lost faith in the promises of life. Let our prayer be for more focused caring communities, a more supportive culture, a more understanding and sympathetic people.

May we be contained and energised by a Faith that gives us a sense of vitality, curiosity, and enrichment.

A Prayer of Evocation

Good Spirit of Life:

Lift us above our uncertainty and our many questions and searching so that we will find something that is really important, something that will make a difference to the way we live, the way we cope, the way we take hold of life.

Let us all be carriers of that Good Spirit of healing and affirmation, of acceptance, and the search for harmony. Let all people be open to the power of a Good Spirit in the world and in people — a Good Spirit that lifts us and strengthens us in all the ways of a good and generous and healing Spirit.

May we find ways that bring a special contentment and wisdom. May we find ways to give of ourselves with generosity and goodness of heart.

Good Spirit of Life:

Touch us at this time with the energies of enthusiasm and renewed hope. Touch us at this time with the energies of healing and renewed inspiration. Touch us at this time with the energies of optimism, persistence and common purpose.

Touch us at this time with the energies of good memories and new inspiration. Touch us today that we will know in the depths of our heart and soul that we are fully accepted and abundantly blessed.

When it is difficult to make sense of our circumstances, keep us searching for a new way to open for us. When we are holding onto the injustice and unfairness of life, keep us believing in a hope that will give strength to the future.

When we are absorbed in our pain, keep us alive to focus on what is yet beautiful in life.

A Prayer of Celebration

We are here that we might find in the quietness our spirits lifted and strengthened by that Good Presence of God. When we are in that Presence we know we will be a different presence to each other.

We celebrate every sign of the Good Presence

in the cherry tree in full bloom

in the innocence and excitement of children at play

in the poetry and stories that give energy to our imagination and inspiration.

We celebrate the recurring signs of goodness in the world

keep open the doorways to wisdom and knowledge

keep open the lifelines of faith, hope and charity

keep us searching for harmony within us and harmony with each other.

We celebrate every day as a special day

the great mysteries of life

the awesome potential of every human being

the astonishing experiences of hope and healing, of courage and compassion.

A Prayer of Gratitude

Let this prayer bring together our gratitude, for the renewal of our courage and consolation, for the strengthening of our hope and faith, for the support and care of many people.

Let this prayer bring together our gratitude for the many pathways that opened to us, for the many gifts that have come to us.

Let our personality be expanded by the Spirit of generosity. Let our personality be enriched by gathering together in this place. Let this place be a strong part of who we are and what we can yet become.

Let the quietness speak strength to our sprits. In the quietness we find healing. In the quietness there is room for hope to be reborn. In the quietness we are lifted to the possibilities of life at its best.

We are grateful for the many gifts that flow into our lives. We are grateful for the flow of relationships that enrich and support us in life. We are grateful for the many pathways that open us to new meanings in life and the constant encouragements to live life fully. We are grateful for the constancy of things and for the expansive surprises:

for great words and great writings

for the words we can speak and the letters we can write

for expansive minds and inspiring personalities

for our searching minds and for the astonishing features of our personality.

A Prayer of Affirmation

Help us to believe in ourselves — in the very best in the human spirit that we may grow towards that best of spirit. Knowing its goodness, its energy, its strength, its resilience.

Help us to build bridges and maintain bridges, bridges that link us to other people and the world

— bridges of education and enlightenment, bridges of hope and courage, bridges of reconciliation and cross cultural growth, bridges of human intelligence and human survival.

Help prevent us from withering:

withering of the spirit

withering in our works of kindness

withering in our generosity.

Prevent us from withering

withering of the mind and body

withering of the intelligence, of searching, of tiredness

withering of traumatic experiences

withering of our arteries and our brains in our soul

withering as an angry, unforgiving, empty closed soul.

Let us be expanded in our spirits:

restored in mind

renewed in body

strengthened in the core of our soul.

A Prayer for Vital Energy

There is within us a continual searching for a vital energy, to lift us into a larger life. There is within us an open window that waits for the wind of a new spirit. There is within us a murmuring motivation to find and re-find the best purposes for our life.

Eternal God let our prayer arouse in us what we can be, what we can do, what we can become.

Source of all our best imagination, of all our best innovation, of our inspiration, may we be infused with that energy and desire to step beyond our safe boundaries and our well-known zones of comfort.

So that we will see new possibilities and have the courage to pursue them, explore our own expanding personality and find the pleasure in owning it. Enable us to rise above destructiveness and become encouragers of a better way.

Help us to be lifted out of our enclosed thoughts and anxieties to be part of our expressive spirit. Lift us out of the small world of our lives to find new strength in a large and helpful faith. Let our compassion and generosity go out to all who have been damaged in childhood.

Let our encouragement go out to all who have become impoverished in their inner being. Let our supportive thoughts bring comfort to all who grieve, and all who ponder what life is to mean for them. Lift us all to be part of a helpful healing spirit, and confirm us in living with optimism and hope.

Help us to keep alive the spirit of active and genuine caring in the world. Help us to notice and acclaim the incidents of active and genuine compassion in the world. Help us to encourage everyone to celebrate their vitality and their inner goodness. Help us to tap into the strengths of a healthy, hopeful life. To make good choices, embrace good words, and bring a good spirit to the world.

A Prayer for Quietness

Our prayers are times when we can set aside our worries and the burdens on our minds. Here is a time to be open to the energy of quietness. May the God who gives the awesome gift of quietness throw the gentle net of that quietness over us.

Gratitude:

And so we are grateful — that in the busiest of times we can pause and discover a new perspective. That in the saddest of times we can pause and discover a new strength. That in those times when things are out of focus, we can pause and discover a new way. We are grateful for the discovery of new strength, a new way, a new faith.

Healing:

In those times when our thoughts are in turmoil may the God who comes with the gift of healing bring that gentle breath of healing to our lives. In those times when there is much anxiety and gloom about the future, and we have pushed aside the gift of gladness at being alive, may we be open to that gentle breath of healing.

In all the burdens of our body and mind, we bring our quietness and gratitude to mingle with that breath of healing.

Hope:

This is our life every day — that the God who comes with the gift of hope will teach us how to hope. May the Spirit of a New Faith be born in us. May the Spirit of a New Faith give us courage to hope.

May the Spirit of a New Faith give us a better way to meet and live through each day.

A prayer of Gratitude and Astonishment

Let our prayer be a whisper of gratitude and astonishment:

that we are alive and we are here

that we come through these doors with trails of many experiences behind us that we are here hoping we will leave this place our inner spirits lifted, strengthened, and ready.

We pray for the God of Life's unfolding moments:

may we recognise the good moments of life

may we be open to the enchanting moments of life

may we be carriers of the expectations of enchantment

may we give our energy to the good and generous moments of life.

Good Spirit May We:

find a quietening strength and stability

find an optimistic attitude in our way of meeting our everyday challenges

find a good sense of hopefulness carrying us into each new day

believe again in the great gifts that are around us every day.

SELECTED READINGS FROM THE SCRIPTURES

Here are words everyone will understand. They express the strong content and meaning of each passage, without attempting to be a literal translation. We can be certain that the original writer of these words did not intend people to spend hours trying to understand every word. We all know as we write our letters to people how one word can be misinterpreted — when the overall content was what was really important. So with these words — allow yourself to flow with the fullness of the content.

We are here talking about a New Faith. Before we discovered this faith, we were living a very constricted divisive life.

But this faith opened us to a new conception of who we are and who we are to be. It lifted us out of our divisions and discriminations.

Everyone has been brought into a new identity, a new way of living, as people who in good faith recognise that what Christ said is possible, is for us to put into effect.

Galatians 3:23-29

This is my prayer: May your love show a greater awareness, and a greater depth of understanding and compassion; and thus you will have a good sense of what is vital.

Philippians 1:9

And so by the stimulus of the ways of Christ, by every incentive of love, and by your owning the good spirit in your life, by your warmth and tenderness.

I pray that you will give me the utter joy of seeing you live in harmony. With strong empathy of heart and soul, you may think and act caringly towards one another, considering one another's needs as much as your own.

Philippians 2:1-3

Now good friends, be strengthened as you feel the good Presence of God.

Let your anxiety fall away, as you focus your minds on the God who is a source of serenity and peace that is beyond your understanding.

Let your heart and mind be lifted into a new life and a new way to be. Always look for the good, the true, and the beautiful — those things that bring out the best.

those things that are really excellent;
that evoke your strongest admiration.
Let your life respond and resound to these things.

Philippians 4:1, 6–9

There is something within us that stretches far out to the God beyond us — to the source of all goodness, the source of our deepest consolation.

We look for some consolation and comfort in all our troubles: and as we know such consolation and comfort, we would want to bring comfort and consolation to others.

The cup of suffering is never far from us. Jesus of Nazareth tasted that cup, but he also reminded us of the other cup that is overflowing with consolation.

Hard to believe when we are in distress, but we do know this: that as we recover our strength, we become powerful carriers of comfort and strength to others. That is the hope that is firmly grounded within us. It is part of the divine gift of life.

2 Corinthians 1:3–5

I have been given the gift of a faith that can transform my life. I know that I carry this gift in a very frail vessel. The transforming comes from a source beyond me — from God and not myself.

In my life I am under stress from every side, but I do not go under; often troubled, but never at my wits' end; though I might feel like one who is frightened, I never feel abandoned; I might be struck down, but I am not destroyed. We might die the death Jesus died, but in His life I see the life we can live. True, while we live we always live under the shadows of death, but we can also live a life that will reflect the life Jesus lived. Part of us is always dying a death, but part of us is also reaching out to the full enjoyment of life.

We believe that we can rise from our life of deadness and come alive to life in all its fullness, and in the courage that Jesus showed we can live as if in his presence. This is the gift we are given, and the more we are aware of this positive word of grace that is around us, the more we feel our thanksgiving wanting to burst forth and be part of the glory of God.

2 Corinthians 4:7-15

We ask God for the best wisdom and understanding so that all we do in life will be truly worthy and acceptable to Him.

Be alive with an active goodness and grow in real depth of wisdom.

May God give you strength, give you ample courage to meet everything that comes, give you the sense of being one of God's people.

Know this, we have been released from our darkened past and now we can be part of a new life knowing that all things come together and are held together by a good faith.

It is a Faith in Jesus Christ's new way — of reconciliation, not just you and the next one, but the whole universe. Imagine being part of a reconciling process, a reconciling experience, and at last finding a peace of heart and mind, in our body and in our blood. For reconciliation is nothing less than that.

Colossians 1:9-20

In the very depths of your being, embrace all the loving energy that flows from the very spirit of Christ the length and breadth, the height and depth of it all.

Thus reach out to the fullness of life, and the comprehensive awareness of the mystery we call God.

Be gentle. Be patient. Be fore-bearing. Be charitable. Look for that union of souls that holds everyone together.

For we are all one body, one Spirit, we all pray to the one God — the God who is over all things, the God who is within us all.

Ephesians 3:18, 4:3-6, 13-16

'Behold I stand at the door and knock.'

Speak directly to all people — they have lost what is vital. They need to take a comprehensive review of everything, and be prepared to open their eyes so that they can see life and the world and the future in a different way. Here is a picturesque metaphor, somewhat over sentimentalised and distorted by the Holman Hunt painting:

Don't you realise — there is someone knocking on your door.

If you hear it and open the door, that Good Presence from without will come within and bring you to the table for a most expansive conversation.

It will be as if the whole universe has been opened to you, and you will sense that our God is at the very centre of life's victorious pathways. Let this Spirit speak to you.

Revelations 3:20-21

I was looking for a new heaven and a new earth, for the old heaven and the old earth had gone, and the sea was dried up.

A new creation was appearing before me, and I heard a voice, and the voice was saying —

Now do you see that there is a Divine Presence right amongst you? It is a Presence that reassures you that you are fully accepted.

All weeping and crying

All anguish and pain

All death and mourning

Lose their hold.

The voice went on to say — you can start again. Everything can become new. Write this down so that you remember —

I am the meaning of all things, from the beginning to the end, A–Z, Alpha to Omega. Let everyone thirsting in the depths of their soul drink from the fountain of life.

Revelations 21:1-6

The whole event and story of Jesus Christ speaks of how special we all are. What a marvellous thing it is that God opens life to us, brings surprises to us, so that we can rediscover a strong hope even in our worst times. It is like a resurrection giving us back our life, after we feel we have lost it.

This is one of the great givens of life: a hope that nothing can destroy or spoil. It is always waiting for us.

In fact, when you realise this gift — you will discover the joy at its depths — even though you know you will continue to have many difficulties. But take heart — just as gold must pass through the assayer's fire, more precious than gold is a strong faith that has stood the test.

It is a faith that brings a new sense of a joy. A faith that keeps alive your search for the expansive wholeness of your soul, where you once again live life to the full, in the here and now.

1 Peter 1:3-9

Here is my appeal to you, the leaders of your community.

Care for the people for whom you have this privilege of being an important part of their lives. Care for them generously, not as if you feel compelled to do it. Do it out of a genuine commitment. Do it freely, setting a good example, never lording it over people: and at the end of the day, you will know it was worthwhile, and your sense of reward will be great.

1 Peter 5:1-4

A BLESSING

May the God you see in all the colours of creation, arouse in you a sense of awe and wonder;

May the God who is a sacred presence be real to you;

May the God who is a source of inspiration and courage, keep calling you forward;

May the God who opens you to the pathways of your best humanity, keep you on those pathways.

ENDNOTE

There is much to be said about a life fully lived and well examined. I trust that this book plays some part in providing a different outlook, an alternative view of older life, and how we might live it more thoughtfully, intelligently, and successfully. In whatever stage of life you are, it is possible to create a more positive and fulfilling life. You can have a life where with just a little faith, hope and love you might thrive and flourish.

ACKNOWLEDGEMENTS

I would particularly like to thank the St Michael's community for their ongoing support and belief in the spiritual and psychological wellbeing of people at all stages of life. My thanks are due also to Dr Coral Brown for her encouragement and contribution to the manuscript, and to Dr Sheila Cameron for her professional editing skills and eye for detail.

ABOUT THE AUTHOR

Dr Francis Macnab is a clinical psychologist specialising in psychotherapy, trauma, self-worth, contextual analysis and older years. He is the author of more than 40 books including *The 30 Vital Years, Don't Call Me Grumpy, Life After Loss* and *The Traumas of Life and their Treatment*. Dr Macnab holds a PhD degree and an honorary Doctorate from the University of Aberdeen. He also has an honorary doctorate from RMIT in psychology and applied science. He founded The Cairmillar Institute in 1961 and is the former president of The International Council of Psychologists and was awarded the Sir James Darling Medal and the Member of the Order of Australia.